52
AMAGING JOURNEYS

by
The Coaches of Journey Fitness

Photos by
Patti Kitchen

Published by

Scriptor
PUBLISHING GROUP

TABLE OF CONTENTS

DEDICATION

As Mark Twain once stated, *"How far we travel in life matters far less than those we meet along the way."* This book is dedicated to the staff and members of Journey Fitness. Thank you for being part of our Journey and allowing us to be part of yours.

AS WE BEGIN

THE JOURNEY THAT BEGAN JOURNEY FITNESS

By Travis and Cyndy Barnes

"For I know the plans I have for you,
plans to prosper you and not to harm you,
plans to give you a hope and a future."

– Jeremiah 29:11

We had been married 11 years, and I was incarcerated for 9 of them. This story could end here and be amazing. Can you imagine the dedication that it took to stand beside someone through almost a decade of incarceration? I will always be eternally grateful for this. Being removed from my wife and daughter was like having a limb removed. I would dream of holding my daughter and wake with tears in my eyes as I realized it was just a dream. I would tell you more about that Journey, how it came to be and how we made it through but that story is another book titled *Journey Fitness*.

For now, I'll just tell you the short version. My wife would drive our daughter 2 hours each way and visit, sometimes twice a week. She accepted an unhappy job in a deli for low pay only because she could have visiting days off. She chose to live with my mother, her mother-in-law, where there were often competing ideas on how to raise our daughter, but it allowed her to spend much of her deli pay on gas to come see me. My wife's family would send her care packages because she could not afford even the shampoo she liked. My wife did everything she could to keep our family together throughout nearly a decade of incarceration. She wrote daily and sent colorings from my daughter. She even sent half-colored drawings so we could color pictures together. She would ask me to draw the face for the pumpkin at Halloween or a treasure map for Easter. Her loyalty and dedication were like nothing I had ever seen or heard of. I couldn't wait to show my appreciation when I came home. I was determined to try to repay her kindness somehow.

I spent my years in prison reacquainting myself with my passion for fitness. I taught adult classes on how to become a certified trainer. I trained people for packages of tuna to eat and stamps to write home. I worked out every day, sometimes twice a day. As soon as I was released, I hit the ground running, working my butt off at a local fitness company. I moved up from trainer to manager to Chief Operations Officer of their multiple locations.

The deli job that my wife had for the last several years was a tough, thankless job in an unhappy environment. As I moved into management, I was able to get my wife a job at this fitness company, which immediately made her more fulfilled. Cyndy is very personable and she found her niche connecting with people and helping them get fit. One small victory was accomplished when I got her out of that miserable job.

The next victory came when I was able to replace the mechanically troubled vehicle that she had been driving to visits. It was a vehicle given to her by a friend and not exactly something you would want for a reliable car. It was a proud day when she drove off the lot in her red Hummer. It was costly, but after all that she had done I could have hired her a limousine to drive her around and it would not have shown my appreciation enough.

Then finally, 2 years after coming home and 11 years of marriage, we purchased our first house. Unfortunately, all of our problems were not behind us. Just 2 months after purchasing our home, we found ourselves in one of the lowest elevations in Pennsylvania for the flood of 2011. Our house was flooded to the second floor. We now had to go from moving into our new home to moving into a FEMA trailer. Our house was almost condemned, so we spent the next year and a half working nights and weekends putting it back together.

We also lost one of our cars in the flood, which made my travel for work very difficult. This fitness company had several locations that I had to travel to and Cyndy worked at the main one. It's the one I would call the home base. With all my traveling, Cyndy and I decided we should buy an inexpensive second car so she would not be without one while I was traveling to other fitness locations. We found a Big Gray Buick for $1,000 from a friend.

On Thanksgiving morning 2012, I drove the car down to our local Turkey Trot where I would lead 80 of our fitness members in the city's annual 5k. The 5k went well. We crossed the finish line and celebrated taking photos with each of our members. I was proud of the community that we had built for this company in just 2 short years. Our team was the largest at the Turkey Trot. As we drove away from the Turkey Trot, the engine made an awful noise, smoke came out and the engine died. I found myself pushing that Big Gray Buick down the road, and it was later determined that it would take a brand-new engine to make it run again.

Now I was in a FEMA trailer, and I no longer had a vehicle of my own. They say bad things come in 3's, and I was hoping they were wrong because I was losing the basics in life, which were a home and car.

Just a few days after the Turkey Trot the owner of our company walked into my office to let me know that my services were no longer needed. I was shocked. My heart sank. It seemed like a final blow. No home, no car, and now, no job.

My departure from the workplace was a bit reminiscent of the movie, *Jerry McGuire,* with Tom Cruise. Tom Cruise's character,

Jerry McGuire, poured his heart and soul into the company where he worked as a sports agent. Jerry McGuire was not just your average employee. He was about changing the company and the world for the better. He stayed up all night to write a memo to the company about how they should have less clients and more focus so that people did not get lost in the shuffle. Jerry McGuire represented what many employees thought but did not dare to say. When he said it, there were high fives from his colleagues, but a plan for his termination from those who cared more about money than ideals. Jerry McGuire was terminated in a busy restaurant so he would not make a scene. He immediately went into survival mode trying to retain his clients, but the company was a step ahead. At the end of the day he had one client left and what seemed like not one loyal colleague left in the world as he said, "I'm leaving. Who's coming with me?" This is when his one admirer, Dorothy Boyd, stood up and said, "I'll go, Jerry," and their adventure to start a new sports agency ensued.

For me it was slightly different. I had co-authored a book and was becoming more the face of the company than the owner. His jealousy was the main reason for my termination, but the day I was terminated it was in the home base location. Cyndy was in the midst of class with a whistle around her neck. When she heard what was happening she immediately took off the whistle and walked out the door with me.

We began unemployment together. Unemployment was not enough to get by so we traveled house to house as traveling trainers. Unemployment, and being a traveling trainer, was not sustainable. We knew we would soon have to find something better and that it might not be in fitness. Around this time, we were invited to check out an empty 1300 sq. ft. space in Elmira, NY. Ray and Rosa Giammichele owned the space. I will never forget walking into that space and seeing all the Christian quotes and hearing the Christian music playing. Rosa was more than a Christian. She was like a Super Christian. She asked what I thought of the place and when I was moving in. To which I replied *"Oh, we are on unemployment, and we don't know anyone in this area."* Then she said, *"That doesn't matter. All I know is God told me you are supposed to be here so when are you moving in?"*

We could have chosen to leave the fitness industry for a more secure job. There were opportunities and we thought about them but in the end, we decided to follow our hearts. As Robert Frost says *"We took the road less traveled and it made all the difference."* Journey Fitness literally began on a wing and a prayer with a landlord willing to wait for payment, an unemployment check, a high-interest loan for equipment, some newspaper advertising on credit and 14 original clients. Just 4 years later, Journey Fitness has 5 locations and over 1200 clients.

Can you believe it? Journey Fitness has impacted thousands of lives! What if I did not go to prison to reestablish my passion for fitness? What if my wife had not supported me? What if we didn't find a landlord who would let us move in with no money? What if we didn't get our first 14 clients? The common thread is that we all followed our hearts and listened to our internal voice. Cyndy did in keeping our family together. I did when I reconnected with my passion for fitness and helping others. I did again when I worked so hard coming home to give my family the life they deserve, and then our landlord did when she listened to her heart.

Travis and Cyndy Barnes

TAKE A JOURNEY

What is your heart saying? Is your heart moving you in a direction? Maybe you have never taken time to listen to your heart. Todd Durkin says *"Figure out the 5 things that make your soul sing. Then say yes to the things that help you do them more often and no to the things that take you away from them."* For me it is Family, Coaching, Speaking, Leading and Travel. What are your answers? Take time today to examine your heart and let love lead you. You just never know where the Journey may lead.

IMPERFECTION

by Wendy Lupo

*"I always find beauty in things that are odd
and imperfect—They are much more interesting."*

– Marc Jacobs

Maybe it's first child syndrome where we're taught, "Make them proud. Do not fail. Please them. Don't be a disappointment."

Sometimes I thought that I should have fought harder or protected myself. Other times I thought that I would rather not talk about it. I'd rather just move on. I silently wondered, "Will anyone love me? How can I ever be happy?"

I never forgot. I was still haunted. I still wondered. I tried to push it away.

Until one day someone asked me, "Do you want to help co-author a book? Oh, and we'd like the authors to tell their stories!" Shite! Tears rolled down my cheeks. How much do I share?

I had always been a people pleaser (do what you think they want, make them happy). I was a focused, organized, hard-working, independent, over achieving, perfectionist! I had a collection of "wonderful" attributes going for me, and yet still continually faced failure, rejection, insecurity, and a low self- image.

It could be because when I was in high school, I didn't feel pretty (being told I should dress differently, wear make-up, do my hair, like my friends). I didn't feel noticed or important, until one day I was. He was much older. I was quiet. I was naive. One night after dating for a bit, he wanted something I wasn't ready to share- not with him, not with anyone. I was only fifteen. I said no. I said no again. I gently pushed away his hands. He wasn't backing down. I gave in, didn't fight for myself, for what I knew was best for me. I was crying. He said it would be fine.

Well it wasn't.

How could I be pregnant? No one could know. I made the decision to have an abortion. It was the only choice. I couldn't shame my family.

Life went on. Only a few people in my life ever knew. How could I ever overcome this failure? Would I ever be successful?

I dove back into perfection mode. I went to college, became a teacher, got a job and then my Master's Degree. I married, had kids and tried to build that traditional family. It failed. Then I tried again, and my second marriage failed.

How was it possible that at work (a classroom teacher) I was confident, successful, not afraid? I had a voice, and it was strong. Yet once outside those elementary doors, I was afraid to take a chance, afraid to try new things, afraid to look in that mirror, afraid to let anyone get close, afraid to think I deserved better. What was wrong with me? This became exhausting. I had to fix it. Things needed to change. I wanted to be happy.

I searched for help at church. My pastor was wonderful. I found a counselor who helped make sense of "me." I read a lot of self-improvement books and inspirational quotes of all types. I did yoga… deep breaths, even tried meditating. I walked. I wrote. I wrote in journals, in notebooks, on scrap pieces of paper. I even tried blogging on the internet, making sure I always kept it in private mode. I bought my second house. I began to run. I ran a lot. I found Journey Fitness. I found strength. Then I found a full hip replacement. I could no longer run. That was tough to face at first, but like we all do, I adjusted.

After years of diving deep into myself, I have realized that my past had such an impact - an impact never faced until many years later. I learned that I can't change the past. I must like myself first, forgive others, forgive myself, and that any failure is growth. We are meant to be human, not perfect, and at times will fall on our face. How we pick ourselves up, dust ourselves off, grow, and move on is what counts! The key is to surround yourself with other humans like yourself- kind, passionate, selfless, supportive, active, simple, earth conscious-nature lovers. Find people who will challenge you, worry about you, laugh and cry with you, see the best in you, see your worst and still love you. That's my circle! My Journey family is a big part of it. Check your circle and who surrounds you.

I know now my past is a piece of me. I have two wonderful children because of it. I am a better person because of it. I continue to be a work in progress. I am still an organized, independent, hard-working individual. I do like myself and even at times am allowing myself to love "me." I am stepping out of my box, bringing my heart with me. Now, I am a personal coach at Journey - building relationships, writing publicly, and even looking in the mirror. I am not perfect, and it is okay. I no longer use the word "failure." Experiences, good and bad, are lessons. Be imperfect. Be resilient. Learn, grow and love.

Take a Journey

"Owning our story can be hard but not nearly as difficult as spending our lives running from it. Embracing our vulnerabilities is risky but not nearly as dangerous as giving up on love and belonging and joy—the experiences that make us the most vulnerable. Only when we are brave enough to explore the darkness will we discover the infinite power of light."

— Brene' Brown, The Gifts of Imperfection

YOUR ADVERSITY IS YOUR ADVANTAGE

By Logan Peters

Have you ever been in a situation that you had little to no control over and it impacted your life in such a way that it changed you forever?

I did. My name is Logan Peters and I have had the honor and blessing to have been a part of some amazing Journeys. These Journeys have been anywhere from extreme weight loss to overcoming drug addiction and to helping people overcome suicidal thoughts. This has been possible through my career as a fitness coach. But, I wasn't always a fitness coach. I, too, have faced some adversity to get to where I am today. It has led to me living my passion of helping people become a better them through health and fitness. I could have never imagined the people I've met along the way and the stories they would share.

Now back to the first question. I only ask this because something like this happened to me. Without this experience, I may have never got to where I am now. It was summer of 2013 and I was in line for a roller-coaster I had ridden many times before. I waited several minutes to get on the ride and when I finally did, it happened. I went to pull down the harness, and it wouldn't click. I tried several times and it just wouldn't give. There I was in front of hundreds of people and being directed off the roller-coaster. This was the most embarrassing moment of my life. I was too overweight to ride the roller-coaster. I was devastated.

That was the moment that changed my life. Here I was, not able to enjoy something I love because of my weight. Worst of all was I had been able to ride it my whole life up to that moment. It was time for a change. That January I was finally able to find the discipline to lose about 100 pounds in 7 months. That's right, only seven months. Some might think this was too fast. I assure you I ate healthy and worked out. I developed a new life style that had to happen for me to enjoy life. It terrifies me to this day to think what might have happened if I never chose to lose that weight. The funny thing is I haven't been back to ride that roller-coaster since!

I learned a lot during my Journey. One thing I learned was I needed to help people find their way as I did. I started to ask, how can I motivate people to change and become a better version of themselves. To help them unveil the greatness within and unleash their true potential. That became my life's mission. Leading me to be a fitness coach. That's what I knew best to help people to my new mission because of where I came from. My part in this book is just another stepping stone in my mission to create great impact.

Take a Journey

Take control of who you are.

This is Just the Beginning

By Jeremy Purifoy

Before   After

I have always struggled with my weight. As an adolescent into my early 20's, my weight always fluctuated I would gain, lose and gain again! My 7th grade year I was cut from the basketball team because I was so out of shape which was my first reality check that I needed to take my health more seriously. I was always an active kid. I grew up right before the technology era so we rode bikes. We had no access to a cell phone. I had to carry 50 cents with me to contact my parents from a pay phone. Throughout high school I played football, basketball, and I spent a lot of time in the weight room. My goal was to continue my football career in college. However, my shoulder said something different. Following my senior year of high school, I had to get arthroscopic surgery on my shoulder. This prevented me from going away to school. In fact, my dad had to drop me off to my previous high school to take night classes for my first semester of college. I was unable to drive and exercise which caused me to go into a state of depression, frustration and lack of motivation. My first semester I put on so much weight and this weight carried throughout my college career.

I continued to turn a blind eye to my weight gain. I worked out every day, lifted weights, my cardio was not up to par but I always knew exercising was important to me. However, just exercising was not cutting it! Nutrition is extremely important. You cannot out train a bad diet. I felt like I was young and could eat and drink whatever I wanted, yet that was not the case. Before I knew it, I was hitting the scale at 270 lbs. In denial, I never thought I would get to this point. I had a vision of myself being a "body builder" - the next Arnold Schwarzenegger. But that was not the case for me. I bulked up and had a lot of muscle but there was more fat covering the muscle. I knew for several years I wanted to get into the fitness industry, I wanted to help people find the best version of themselves. However, when I looked in the mirror at my reflection, I thought if I was a client of myself I would not want to pay the guy looking back at me. I would not have been happy with where my money was going. I wanted to inspire people! I wanted people to say, "I want to look like you!" The realization came to me when I could not find a decent picture of myself for a Facebook profile picture. I just kept clicking through with disgust at how bad I looked, and I struggled with the fact that I recently just noticed how bad it really was. This was a game changer for me. If I wanted to become a personal trainer I knew I had to look the part.

I graduated from college at the age of twenty-four. Following graduation, I knew it was time to make a change. I started meal prepping and upped my cardio game during my workout regimen. I meal prepped every Sunday and Wednesday for the week. Doing this and incorporating cardio I dropped 50 lbs rapidly. In January of 2014 I got my first fitness job at Grand Central Fitness. I was super pumped to finally start my fitness career. However, it was a short stay! In February 2014, Grand Central Fitness burned down! I was supposed to head in to work that morning. I received a phone call at 4:30am informing me that there was no need to come in and to turn the news on. It was a pretty traumatic time. I did not know what to do next. I was about to be a father for the first time. I started questioning myself whether fitness was really for me. My daughter, Jocelyn, was born in March, and I was working solely at the Glove House which is a program for troubled youth. Although it paid the bills, it was not my calling and I was not happy with where I was in my life. My weight loss became stagnant. I hit a plateau at 220-215.

I could not break that 215 mark. In April, I received a phone call from Travis Barnes offering me an internship at Journey Fitness. At this point Journey Fitness was relatively new. Prior to my job at Grand Central I contacted Travis in November 2013, asking if they had any openings. My girlfriend Kristen's, step-mother was a member and she told me about the program and how much she loved it. She suggested that I should apply there to be a coach. It took a while for me to convince myself to contact Travis. When I finally established enough courage to message him it was too late. They just hired a few coaches on, but he did tell me he would keep me in mind for the future. Five months later I received the phone call that would jump start my fitness career.

Since Journey Fitness, as a Coach, I have lost 35 lbs which brought me to a total of 87 lbs lost on my own weight loss Journey. Journey Fitness has been such a blessing. In my time, here I have done more than I would have ever expected. Not even a year in, I helped open Journey Fitness' second location in Corning, New York with very little to no experience. I have never been in a management position. This was all new to me, but I was ready to take on the challenge. I have grown this location with a strong team and awesome dedicated members. Some of those people you will read about in this book. My personal growth as a coach, mentor and leader has come so far, and this is just the beginning. I owe so much to Travis and Cyndy Barnes for taking a chance on me to grow their brand. I would also like to shout out my Corning Team for being the rockstars that they are and making

Journey Fitness Corning such a success. To my members thank you for your dedication. If it was not for you, Journey Fitness Corning would not exist! Again, this is just the beginning. Keep your eyes open on what is to come next!

TAKE A JOURNEY

Never stop learning and growing.

LET YOUR HEART
BE YOUR GUIDE

By Jesse King

I once heard that it's been estimated on average our brains produce as many as 60,000 thoughts per day. Interestingly about seventy to eighty percent of those thoughts are either negative, or completely bogus.

I have also heard that ninety percent of what we worry about will never happen, and the other ten percent of our worries we can't do anything about anyway. So why worry, right?

Based upon these insights, it's no wonder I've found a major obstacle in my life to be none other than myself. Daily I struggle with the infamous "stinking thinking." I can think of many examples from my past, but there's one memory that stands out a little more than others. Why? Because this experience taught me the value of defining your purpose in life, the value of following your heart, and a very important lesson in perseverance. When you get knocked down by life, get up, and keep moving forward.

It was a hot and humid August morning. I was drenched with excitement. My emotions were all over as I drove up Route 13 eagerly on my way to Ithaca College. I was headed there to play football and attend pre-season training camp. The opportunity to play college football was like a dream come true. This moment was something I fantasized about since junior high, and something I worked my butt off for during my high school football career.

Ironically, I did not take my college football experience very seriously. I showed up to pre-season training camp unprepared and even worse, injured. As a result, I found myself on the sideline just a week into training camp. Physically, I was hurt. Eventually part-way through the season I was ordered to have a knee scope to fix the issue. Mentally though, I was worse off and headed down a path of self-destruction.

The enthusiasm I had for playing college football was very short lived. While I rehabbed my knee injury, my attitude shifted and became dismal. I started to believe I would never receive any playing time. Although there was no reason for me to think that, stinking thinking led me to believe it anyway. My stinking thinking literally began choking the life out of the dream I had been pursing since junior high. Consequently, I counted myself out before I even started to try. My true failure at this moment was failing to realize that when you're down, the only place left to go is up.

Blind to the possibilities around me, my perspective on life became grimmer. I stopped caring about school, and my grades started to suffer. Eventually when I was cleared to play football, the bulk of the season had passed, and lo and behold my passion for the sport I loved was completely gone!

Looking back, I recognize a major factor contributing to my poor attitude during the football season, an absence of hope. I had no vision to keep me focused through the tough times. My dreams lacked inspiration. And when your dreams don't inspire you, it's easy to fall off track.

At the end of the season I decided my football career was over, and subsequently I didn't care. But it was here in this delicate moment as a freshman in college I received an epiphany. My parents may have jumpstarted the message by reminding me college is way too expensive not to care, but aside from their concern, the message from my epiphany was clear. I was created for a greater purpose. If I follow my heart, I will always feel satisfied.

Rejuvenated, I began listening intently to my heart, eager to see where it would lead me. I felt as if I were becoming in tune with my inner coach. My inner coach was telling me to get up, and keep moving forward. What a valuable life lesson. No matter how hard you fall, get up, and keep moving forward.

I finished one semester at Ithaca College and transferred. It was a difficult decision, but I am thankful that I did it. I believe transferring gave me the opportunity to regroup and focus on my saving grace - exercise!

A few years later I earned my Bachelor's degree in Exercise Physiology from SUNY Brockport. Then I earned my strength and condition certification. Also, I am proud to say I recently celebrated my three-year anniversary as a personal coach at Journey Fitness. But even more important than all my achievements would be the clarity I've gained on my life's purpose.

I believe my passion for exercise led me to defining my purpose in life. My purpose is to serve others by adding value in any way possible. But here is the key point. I need to first value myself before I can add value to someone else. Therefore, I have found it necessary to do the following two things:

1) Overcome stinking thinking with personal development. Personal development is a broad term so I like to think of it as learning the necessary skills and developing the necessary habits I need to be the best version of me.

2) Embrace the call to action set forth by life and embark on the lifelong Journey of becoming a successful leader. According to leadership expert, John C. Maxwell, "Leadership is not about titles, positions, or flow charts. It's about one life influencing another." I like that explanation because I feel it helps me make the connection between my passion for exercise, my purpose, and leadership.

In closing, sometimes in life we get knocked down. It's inevitable. Just like the flow of negative thoughts, and false worries occurring in our mind, it's inevitable. But, ultimately, it's our choice how we react to it. I use my college football experience as an example of how the end of one thing can be the beginning of something totally new and wonderful. The take home message is to not let negativity, or stinking thinking influence your choices. Rather let your heart be your guide. I agree with William Jennings Bryan when he said that "Destiny is not a matter of chance, it's a matter of choice. It's not a thing to be waited for, it's a thing to be achieved."

Furthermore, make the choice today to let your heart guide you to the beautiful destinations that can be found in your tomorrows.

TAKE A JOURNEY

Where does 'stinking thinking' show up in your life? What are some of the ways you can 're-think' those ideas? Make the choice to follow your heart.

SHAKE UP

By Jeff Case

"When Life shakes you up, you've gotta shake back."

– JC

Sometimes in life you get shaken up.

It was Christmas time. People were joyful, grateful and giving. I was excited. Christmas time is my favorite time of the year, or at least I thought. It also meant that my best friend from high school would be home for his annual Christmas visit from college. I remember getting in my car and driving to see him as soon as he arrived home. I knocked on the door. He opened it and I rushed him like a defensive end to the quarterback. We exchanged greetings. And then the three words that would "give" me the "reason for the season" so to speak, and send me on my Journey for the next year were spoken, "Man, you look disgusting." Has anyone you loved or admired ever said something so blatant to you?

At the time, I laughed. Not really bothered by the words. I mean I knew I let myself go. I had all the excuses - working three jobs to support my newly wedded wife and our son. I didn't have time for the gym, me, or my family for that matter. I would work and sleep. It was terrible. Does this sound familiar?

That whole week he was home, I heard it from him every day, "Man, you look disgusting!" One of those days, I edged out, "What do you mean?" Without hesitation he said to me, "I've never seen you like this before. It's disgusting man. You have a wife and a son to take care of and you're looking like that?" He left for school right before the New Year, just after my 24th birthday.

So, in January of 2011, I decided to start my Journey to a better me by changing my mindset to getting better every day. Each day I wanted to get better than the one before for my family and my relationships. At 280 pounds for the past two years, I was pretty secluded in my sweat pants and hoodies. I had people close to me that never even knew I was that heavy. I just decided that I wasn't going to end where I was. I knew what was within me. I had something more important than excuses, I had patience. I knew I could become who I knew I was. I began that first early morning with a walk. The next day was a longer walk, then a jog, then a mile and another and another. I soon was on track with something that started as small steps that built momentum. It became a compound effect. After 21 days, healthier choices became a habit instead of a yo-yo affect. I cut out the carbs and sugars ninety percent of the time while enjoying my ten percent on the weekend. I felt so much better than I did before. I was more productive for my family and for myself. I went on to lose   110 lbs. in just over a year's time. I went from 280 lbs. of sick, thick, and tired, to 170 lbs. of energy and strength. I did this through dedication in exercise and consistent healthy food choices.

But sometimes in life you get slammed too.

Flash-forward to June 2014 through January 2015, my wife's Grandmother passed away. I was about to take the field for kick-off for my football game when I received the call. I was close to her because I was taking care of her full time in our home over the past three years. On top of that I was out of a job which sent me into a time of emotional eating. I began to put some weight back on. At first five, then ten, and then feeling like I was drowning again. I did find a new job installing gutters and that was going well for a few months until I fell 20 feet from a ladder on a job site and sprained my ankle to the point where I could not walk for over three months. I crawled from room to room in pain tending to my children while my wife was going to college full time. I felt down on myself because I was very active and now I couldn't even stand up let alone exercise. Soon, the bad eating habits crept back in. From June through the new year, I went from 175 pounds to over 200 pounds and I felt terrible. I was looking for a glimpse of hope because my ankle was taking so long to heal. It wasn't until January of 2015 that I could stand for more than a few minutes without my ankle throbbing. That is when I began exercising and eating better again. By March of 2015, three months later, I was back down to 170 lbs. with over 30 lbs. lost.

This makes becoming a coach a very deep, valuable and meaningful experience to me. I want to share my story to help encourage others to make positive and healthy changes in their lives so that we don't have to live sick, thick, and tired anymore. Sometimes in life we get shaken up. Sometimes we get slammed. Every day is an opportunity to shake back, to slam back at life and decide to be a part of the solution rather than the problem. As a coach, I want to impact and inspire others to take action, lose fat, build muscle, and feel better so that we can become better versions of ourselves and build stronger, healthier relationships in life. Never let a stumble in the road be the end of your Journey. I believe that everyone needs a coach in life and that's what I set out to be every single day!

Jeff Case — Before AND After

TAKE A JOURNEY

Sometimes what we're given in life might not seem pleasant at the time but is just what is needed to make a change worth telling a story about.

"Make the rest of your life, the best of your life."

— Eric Thomas

GET COMFORTABLE BEING UNCOMFORTABLE

By Nicole Wilber

"Life begins at the end of your comfort zone."

– Neale Donald Walsch

Have you ever done something that totally scares the crap out of you? Something you never, in a million years, would imagine yourself doing? Do you avoid doing things because you're afraid? Maybe you're uncomfortable? It's time to get comfortable, being uncomfortable. I grew up as your typical,

41

straight A student. I did all the things my older sister did, because that's what was expected. We were both dancers, gymnasts, and cheerleaders. Sure, dance competitions and gymnastics meets were quite nerve-wrecking, but my sister had always done it, so I knew what to expect.

My life has always been very structured and scheduled; I would certainly never be described as a spontaneous person. Like many people, I was always a, "someday" type of person. Someday I'll visit that place. Someday I'll run that race. Someday I'll zip-line. Someday I'll skydive. My 'someday' list, or my bucket list, started to grow longer and longer.

I still don't know exactly what it was that clicked, but something did. I finally just said to myself, "What the heck am I waiting for?" The next thing I did? I called and made a skydiving appointment for my dad and me. With my pride, there was no backing out at that point. Sure enough, when I was 23 and my dad was 54, we went skydiving for our first time. The thrill was amazing. I have always loved rollercoasters and other thrill rides, but this was like no other. To me, this was an accomplishment. See, I always held the mindset, work now play later. I always thought I had to have a stable career, buy a house, have a family, save tons of money, and then, only then, I could enjoy the fruits of my labor and chip away at my bucket list. When that something clicked, though, things changed. I have always loved the Robert Frost poem, "Stopping by Woods on a Snowy Evening." More specifically, the ending that says "miles to go before I sleep." This always resonated with me. To me, it meant that I had a lot of things I wanted to do before it was too late. If I kept pushing my bucket list off until 'someday,' then someday it might be too late.

I finally began doing those things. That same year, I also ran my first half marathon and participated in my first Tough Mudder obstacle course. All of these were checks on my bucket list. I have taken many trips now that I previously would have been hesitant to go on.

I firmly believe that if I had not adopted this new "take action now" mindset, I would never have stumbled across Journey Fitness. I was so nervous to stray away from the job I was comfortable doing for the last 10 years, waiting tables. I was a certified personal trainer for a year and a half before I even applied for my first fitness job. A friend approached me about Journey Fitness, and with my new mentality, I said to myself, what am I waiting for? I am beyond grateful I decided to take that leap. I have had the opportunity to build relationships with some of the most incredible people along my Journey. I cannot begin to describe the growth and transformation that has taken place within me since coming to Journey Fitness. I am thankful every day for each member and every teammate I've been blessed to work with.

I now find myself to be much more adventurous and even spontaneous at times. My childhood was amazing growing up, but I am thankful I broke free from my previous mentality of 'work hard now, play later.' I do something every day that makes me happy and fulfilled. I have now been to places I never thought I'd have a chance to see. I have completed 2 half marathons and 4 Tough Mudders, the 4th one being the best one yet. This is when my fiancé, Josh, proposed to me. Since we have been together I feel I have influenced him to come out of his comfort zone as well. We completed his first half marathon together, first Tough Mudder, first skydive, and many other adventures, with many more to come. I look forward to continuing to help each other grow and venture further and further away from our comfort zones, together.

TAKE A JOURNEY

The point is, don't wait. The time is never perfect. Enjoy life now, while you still can, because someday may never come. Often times people get so caught up in the busy-ness of life that we put off the things we genuinely enjoy doing and before we know it, we find ourselves feeling unfulfilled. Always make time for family and those special moments that will turn to memories. Work hard, play hard, every day.

A Crown of Sweat with a Soul on Fire

By Ambir Case

"The most dangerous woman of all is the one who refuses to rely on someone else's sword to save her because she has her own."

– r.h. Sin

S truggle. Who doesn't know it? I am a true believer that you cannot believe your struggles to be "worse" than others. Every person goes through trials. No matter how seemingly perfect someone's life seems to be, I can assure you, it is not. It's how you choose to react to the things that negatively impact you, how you rise from them, that determines you as a person. We can make excuses or we can give effort. I can say this with confidence because I have been on both sides of the fence, the excuses and the effort.

Growing up, born and raised in Elmira, New York, I lived a pretty normal life… (whose life is normal?) I participated in a variety of sports including the "boys" wrestling team. However, soccer was my true love! I was always active, staying outside until my parents would whistle for us to come in when the street lights came on. I never struggled with weight, never had to be conscious of the foods I ate.

In 2012, I was blessed to welcome my beautiful little girl, Adilynn, into my life. During my pregnancy I again, never worried about what I ate or weight. I had been so active that I was confident the weight would just fall off. Diagnosed with gestational diabetes during this time, I still kick myself in the butt and take full responsibility for that happening. Nutrition is vital. I had never been so depressed in my life than during this time. I felt terrible about myself. I lived in sweat pants and t-shirts. I was embarrassed of myself. I didn't love myself and that is no way for anyone to live. Needless to say, the weight did not come off. I kept assuring myself it would happen and after a year and a half of it not happening, I was finally honest with myself. You can only call baby weight, "baby weight" for so long. It was time to step up and make a change versus an excuse. I decided to begin my Journey.

I could talk about the tears and frustration I battled during my Journey from beginning to end, but the truth of the matter is, it never ends. My Journey is still in progress. Just know it was hard, it was difficult but it was worth it. I didn't make a few changes, I made a life change. I got my workout in every single day, it was not an option but a priority. My nutrition did a 360, from whatever I wanted to eat to meal prepping on Sundays so I was prepared for success in my work week. Within 9 months I managed to lose all of my baby weight and then some, around 45 pounds. During this time I was overwhelmed by the number of women, mothers, who reached out to me wanting to know how, what I did, what they could do, could I help them. I realized I wanted to help. I wanted to help these women to not feel a way that they don't deserve. I realized I would do anything to make sure women never felt the way I had about myself, that I wanted them to know they're beautiful, that they can do it and most importantly they are worth it. I began holding groups that other women and I would post in daily, doing workouts, sharing meal ideas, helping one another. Then I found Journey Fitness.

I have made so many relationships and look forward to the Journeys I still have yet to be a part of!

During my time at Journey I created a new goal - to not only inspire and motivate others, but to build muscle and gain strength. Twenty pounds up, I am the strongest and in the best shape I have ever been. It is a mental battle every day to not focus on the scale number as it is with everyone, but again, it is just a number. I am told consistently how much I have motivated other women, mothers, and how much they look up to me. What they don't realize is all of the women I know inspire and motivate me. They're the reason I do what I do. They help keep me accountable because I don't want to fail them. I am inspired to inspire so that my daughter grows up surrounded by strength - physically, mentally, and emotionally - so she can be so much more than I will ever be. I do not ever want her to question her beauty or rely on someone else for her worth.

So to all of you – yes, you - thank YOU for being MY motivation!

TAKE A JOURNEY

You never have to rely on anyone else to determine your own self-worth. You deserve to feel good and to know that you are beautiful, both inside and out.

FROM RED TO YELLOW TO GREEN

By Kurtis Hall

Growing up I was supported in everything I did by my parents and grandparents. I was encouraged to be better and to push myself to my limits. They would go to any extreme to get me where I was the best as an athlete, including late nights, early mornings, long drives, and many hours at the field just watching and cheering. They taught me to remember others and treat others how I wanted to be treated, but in my mid-teens I lost track of others. I got yellow and/or red cards game after game and was willing to do anything to the top dog even at the expense of others. My senior year of high school I got refocused and starting treating people with respect but I had a huge uphill battle to regain the respect of all those I disrespected and mistreated for years.

Since graduating, I have realigned my focus to helping others be the best possible version of themselves. I am now married with two beautiful children and am always learning the balance between self-focus which is important and my focus on others. There is nothing more satisfying in life than helping others – spiritually, mentally, emotionally and physically – be the best them. I believe that we can accomplish much more as whole beings, and I will always have a passion to help others and invest in the next generation.

TAKE A JOURNEY

What do you need to do to be your best, mentally, emotionally and physically? When you consistently improve in those areas, you accomplish more and will, ultimately, live a better life.

BUILD MUSCLES
INSTEAD OF SCARS

By Destiny Barnes

Destiny Barnes has encountered many things at the young age of 15. Her father was incarcerated for almost 10 years of her life. In addition to that, her past includes sexual assault, rape, substance abuse and attempted suicide. Destiny could easily have chosen to consider herself a victim and let life pass her by. Instead, she has chosen to see herself as a survivor. Destiny has chosen to let her past build muscles rather than scars.

Read on and you will find Destiny's story at the end of this book. In that chapter, Destiny shares her pain and her story of overcoming. Recently, Destiny joined the Journey Fitness Team so she can better dedicate her life to helping others. If you are moved by Destiny's story then please donate to www.imatterfoundation. com for the prevention of teen suicide and self-harm.

TAKE A JOURNEY

We all have challenging experiences in life. It is up to us to decide whether we will let those challenges become scars or muscles. Take a moment to define your own challenges and consider how you can use those experiences to get stronger and, perhaps, as Destiny is doing, use them to help others.

LOOK BETTER

PUT YOURSELF FIRST
–YOU HAVE TO LEAD FROM THE FRONT

By Travis Barnes

Resa Ike and her husband, RC

"To lead others, you must first lead yourself."

– John Maxwell

Resa was in a constant state of worry. She couldn't sleep. She refused to participate in family events and struggled to do things with her children. She felt unable to experience life. The reason for this was that she was obese.

Have you ever heard someone say they are carrying baby weight after having a baby? Well 12 years ago Resa carried triplets as a surrogate for her sister. She would tell everyone that she could not lose weight because having triplets messed her up. She would put others ahead of herself not really knowing that it was so she could ignore her own condition.

Then she came to Journey Fitness. Resa had been at Journey Fitness for a while still believing she could not lose weight, and she remembers when it was that her thinking changed. She was talking with Logan, one of the Journey Fitness coaches, and he told her *"Her mistakes were going to be their mistakes together and that they would have to fix them together so if she ate something wrong or didn't feel like going on then he would redirect her. He said no mistake was too big to fix. He kept telling her that she mattered. Her life was just as important as all the other people she takes care of, and to always put herself first."* That's when Resa realized she mattered.

The new Resa changed how she interacted with her family. Prior to starting her Journey she was a servant to their needs. Everyone's needs were ahead of her own, so much so, that her newfound relationship with Journey Fitness created some tension in her relationships at home. She seemed obsessed with Journey and because she was putting herself first, her family felt neglected. It's important to note that your loved ones may not always understand you but they will always love you. If you show them something is important to you long enough, then those who love you will find a way to support you. It wasn't long before Resa's family saw the weight loss and were proud of what she was doing. They decided to follow her lead and join Journey Fitness. Resa was now a leader to her family instead of a servant. Both her husband and her daughter were now part of her Journey. Her husband, RC, said "We have always done so much together that it only seemed right that I joined Journey Fitness to do this with her as well"

Three months after RC joined Journey Fitness, Resa achieved her long-term goal losing over 100 pounds. Five months after RC joined, he achieved his own weight loss goal of 50 pounds. Together they have lost over 150 pounds.

Resa says, *"This Journey was the toughest thing I have ever done but the reward was 100% worth it. I understand that I am valuable and that I am never going back."*

Resa   RC

TAKE A JOURNEY

Do you put others ahead of yourself? Is it because you want them to feel important or because you don't feel important enough? Do you stay focused on what you can do for others so that you don't have to focus on what you can do for yourself? Remember if we don't take care of ourselves then we won't be around to take care of anyone else. Think of this story and realize when you put your health first you may inspire your family to change their health for the better.

Take action today: *Maybe there has been someone who loves you but does not understand your Journey. Don't stay in conflict. Invite them to be part of it.*

SICK AND TIRED OF BEING SICK AND TIRED

By Wendy Lupo

"Nothing happens, until the pain of remaining the same, outweighs the pain of change."

— Arthur Burt

Chris Baxter

"How did I get back here again?" Chris asked herself, as she stared at the anniversary picture of she and her husband in her hand. Chris had reached her fifties. Yikes, fifty! That number haunted Chris as it does many. What does over-the-hill mean anyway? Some define it as being past our prime, old, and no longer useful or attractive! Must we conform to that mentality? Chris wasn't having it!

After having her son and not shedding the weight she had gained in pregnancy, Chris fell into that vicious life cycle of working too hard with a stressful job, coming home too tired to cook, ordering out, sitting around, going to bed, and repeating. Oh, she dieted and lost weight over the years but only to gain it all back and more. She kept sizes 6 to 2x hanging in her closet just in case she couldn't keep the weight off. She took all sorts of exercise classes and tried every diet out there. With no one really keeping her accountable and Chris not one to be a self-motivator, her success was always short lived.

In 2013, on top of everything else, Chris had to have neck surgery. Getting healthy was only going to become more difficult as time went on. With the combination of not liking what she saw in the mirror, constant migraines, rising triglycerides, and the need for medication, Chris knew she needed to take action now. She needed a permanent change.

Friends introduced Chris to Journey Fitness. She was committed to doing what they asked of her. She had witnessed what other members had accomplished so she knew it was possible. She journaled, followed a low-carb diet, and worked out three times each week. In nine months, she had lost forty-five pounds, reaching her set goal. "What was different about Journey Fitness?"

you may ask. Chris will tell you it would be the weekly goals and weigh-ins, the encouragement of trainers and support of her 6:30 a.m. group "family".

So how has life changed for Chris? Her daily life pattern has changed. With the support of her family, she now begins her day with energy, is mindful of what her pantry holds, plans out meals, prepares meals herself (with take-out being a rarity). She walks in the evening, gets good sleep and repeats. Chris is now in maintenance mode, which she will describe as the most difficult part of the Journey. But there are many motivators to keep her on track. She can now get in and out of the family boat all by herself and looks great for any upcoming reunions. Her doctor's visits are much less frightening with news of normal triglycerides, "good" cholesterol in the fifties, and rarely reports of having a head-ache let alone a migraine. Chris describes a time after her weight loss. The family was looking through old vacation photos. They found a picture of her husband and herself. Chris described herself as being so overweight in the picture that when her son looked at it his words were "oh my". He couldn't believe she had been that big. His reaction resonated with Chris. She says, "that's enough to motivate anyone" to maintain a good healthy lifestyle. These days, Chris is no longer embarrassed to look in the mirror. She now embraces the mirror. She is proud of the person looking back at her.

Chris Baxter Now

TAKE A JOURNEY

Don't give up! It won't be easy. It will require change, commitment, and hard-work, but it will be worth it. We only get one life so make the most of your time.

You Are the Sum of Your Choices

By Logan Peters

"If you are willing to do only what's easy,
life will be hard. But if you are willing to do
what's hard, life will be easy."

– T. Harv Eker

Have you ever found yourself doing the same thing over and over because life just seemed to be working that way, even if it was at the expense of your own health and happiness? Lori found herself sitting in the same recliner, wearing the same pajamas, watching the same TV, with a bottle of soda in one hand and a bag of chips in the other.

This was her nightly routine. She was too uncomfortable with herself to go anywhere or do anything. On top of it all Lori had been battling with MS (Multiple Sclerosis) for almost 17 years, she had a recent scare of a possible stroke, and was told by her doctor that she had a fatty liver. In the midst of it all Lori still found that she was committed to this nightly routine because it was easy.

Finally, something clicked and made her think. These bad choices were going to lead her down a path that ends with an early death which would mean she wouldn't have the opportunity to see her children marry and have grandchildren. Lori in that moment had to ask herself, "How much is too much and when am I going to make the commitment to change my ways and get healthy?"

Even after her a-ha moment, it still took her almost a month before starting her Journey to a better lifestyle. She was afraid. Joining a health club was something that made her second guess herself. She was afraid that she wouldn't be able to do anything, that she would embarrass herself, and that no one would look like her. Being judged was the last thing she needed after years of beating herself up for the way she looked.

Lori will tell you that if it wasn't for two of her friends that were already members at Journey Fitness, she might never have walked through those doors. Through support and encouragement Lori participated in that first class. It wasn't easy for her, and she was very sore for the next couple of weeks, but she couldn't give up. She knew she had found something special.

When Lori started her Journey, she was at the heaviest weight in her life. Six months later, she was 60 pounds lighter and feeling better than ever! Lori adapted a new routine that included three workouts each week, weighing in no matter what (even if she knew it wasn't going to be good), and attending a weekly nutrition talk. No longer was the recliner a comfort zone.

Still there was more...Lori started to notice that not only did her weight change but the world around her changed as well. Work seemed to get a little bit easier with her new improved attitude. She now wanted to be active and get out and do things. She even started shopping for clothes again. With her new confidence Lori says, "I worked too damn hard for the results I'm seeing and the way I'm feeling to go back to my old ways!" On top of it all Lori received the best compliment thus far when her husband who she's known for 30 years, said he felt like they were dating again because her attitude had changed so much!

What was hard for Lori in the beginning ended up making her life much easier. She could have continued the way she was and never made the change. That would have been the easy way out. That wasn't good enough for her. Although she will never be free from MS and the threat of an escalation of that disease looms in the darkness, Lori knows she is doing everything she can to make sure her health is at its best.

TAKE A JOURNEY

You are the sum of your choices. What habits do you need to do less of, and what habits do you need to do more of? Identify the routines which you'd like to eliminate or start doing that would improve your health, mind, and body. Then take action today.

MY WHY

By Jeremy Purifoy and Danielle Carro

"Every setback is a setup for a comeback."

– Joel Osteen

I woke up, got the kids around for school and got myself ready for work. I arrived for work like I normally did, with a smile on my face ready to take on the day, when suddenly my morning took a traumatic turn for the worse. I was let go from my job. I had no understanding on why this was happening to me. I played by the rules! Every review that I had nothing ever indicated that this would happen to me. My emotions were so dismantled. I could not hold it together. Everything I worked so hard for was gone with a blink of an eye. I guess I was not a good fit for the position anymore which was incredibly hard for me to hear because I poured my heart and soul in to my work every day. I have become so close to several of my co-workers and now I will no longer be with them. This is hard to swallow!

Let's rewind to the beginning of my Journey. Walking through Journey Fitness doors for the first time I had a little confidence and had originally set my goal at 25 lbs. because I did not think I could do any better! A coach at Journey pushed me to set the bar higher than my expectations and to set a goal to lose 50 lbs. My response was not positive. I told her I would never be able to do that. I was overweight. I ate fast food consistently. Ice cream and sweets were in my everyday routine. I did not have the self-confidence, strength, motivation or the passion to accomplish such an immense goal. I will never forget walking through the door in my oversized shirts and sweats with my hat on, literally hiding myself, like I usually did. For many years my children have been my shield. I would always hide behind them in pictures. I avoided clothes that I knew would make me look awful, and activities where I would perform poorly. I dodged the summer months as much as possible. I have not owned a pair of shorts in many years, and a bathing suit was not going on my body unless it was necessary for my kids. My motivation to change is my kids. I saw that I was sending them down the same path of poor eating habits and living a sedentary lifestyle. I wanted to be a better role model for them and to improve my life. My father passed away at the young age of 67 and my mom has had four strokes and was paralyzed before she turned 68. I wanted to break this vicious cycle of an unhealthy lifestyle and live a longer life for my kids and, hopefully, my future grandchildren.

Having a workout buddy and friend was key for me. It made joining Journey Fitness easier by having an accountability partner. We kept each other motivated, on track with our eating, and pushed each other on a daily basis. Together, Lisa and I have managed to lose weight and become more fit. We are stronger women, and we have found ourselves through this process. Most of all, the Journey Family has been such a huge contributor to my success. Without Journey, this would have never been possible. The people that have become close friends, the coaches and the fit fam, they make it easy to find your confidence, and most importantly, they make fitness fun. The coaches understand their members. They know everyone on a first name basis, their goals, their interests, what motivates them and they know their struggles and helps each person, whether individually or as a team.

Fast-forward to my termination! The result of this situation set me back on my Journey. My Journey in life! My Journey in fitness! This was a challenging time in my life. The months following my termination have been extremely difficult for me, and I can admit that I had given up on myself and lost a huge amount of confidence. This affected so much of my life as a wife, mother, friend, sister and daughter I just felt so defeated. I struggled to get back on my feet. I needed my life back. I needed to be the Danielle that I knew I could be and once was before the storm hit! I took several months off from my fitness routine working two jobs and supporting my family. I did not have the time to get my workouts in which caused the vicious cycle of putting some weight back on. I could not find the motivation or the energy to get back into Journey Fitness. This led to me having to cancel my account. However, the Journey Fitness Corning Team never gave up on me. They stayed in contact with me during my hardship. Whether through text or social media I was always connected. After several months of feeling down on myself I have finally found a job that allows me to pay for my membership and it is close to Journey. Now I am finally ready to get back into training and get the person back that I was prior to this incident. Even though I lost my way, I cannot wait to find my way back. I realize that the months that I was absent from Journey Fitness have changed me drastically but I am ready to learn even more about myself through this Journey!

One word? Hmmm… I have two words; determination and confidence. I did not have either of these when I started but now I have found them. As I go through each workout my determination and confidence increases. I discovered the determination to do better and as the determination started paying off, my confidence grew tremendously. My family, friends, and kids all see the change

in me. I no longer have to hide in a picture. I wear clothes that make me feel good. No matter the number on the scale, it is all about being confident in your own body. I am not perfect. I still worry about that number. I still stress eat and lose confidence. But overall, I am in a much better place, mentally and physically. My kids are all about healthy living and helping me to better myself as a mom and role model each and every day. My lifestyle change has made an impact on my children. They are healthier and more active because of my Journey which will never end.

Take a Journey

Find your why! Let that be what motivates you to come out on top. Persistence and dedication eventually will pay off. It is a Journey never a destination! Always strive for more!

BELIEVE

By Travis Barnes

*"I can do all things through Christ
who strengthens me."*

– Philippian's 4:13

One of life's greatest blessings happens when we find a companion to go through life with. Mary and her husband had been married over 30 years. They were best friends. They went four wheeling together. They would go camping together. They did everything together. Then her husband caught pneumonia. Despite the doctor's best efforts, Mary lost her husband on Sunday March 31st, 2013. After losing her husband, Mary fell into a state of depression and with the depression came weight gain.

One day Mary was hit with a harsh realization that she was 100 pounds overweight. She thought to herself, "If I don't do something about my weight soon then my sons won't have either of their parents left." Mary felt the effects of being obese, and she was very embarrassed by her weight. She hated herself. She was

73

depressed. But Mary was a woman of faith and something told her to join Journey Fitness. Mary listened to that voice and put her trust in Journey Fitness to help her.

This still did not stop her insecurities. She still took extra precautions to make sure that only certain coaches weighed her in. The door to the weigh in room was always shut, and Mary made sure all paperwork was put away when she was finished weighing in. This was done so there could be no chance that anyone could possibly see her weight. Mary was also very cautious to never try any exercises on the floor. She did all her exercises standing. She said "If I get down on the floor I will end up looking like a turtle stuck on its back."

As the weight came off, Mary began to learn that physical changes bring psychological changes. Not only was Mary losing weight, her depression was lifting as well. This gave her a new zest for life. She began to embrace the Journey Fitness community. When Journey Fitness would have their weekly nutrition classes, Mary would even prepare low carb recipes and bring them to share with her Journey Fitness family.

One important breakthrough came when Mary did her first exercise on the floor. It was a proud moment when Mary got down on the floor to do a push up. She says, "It brought tears to my eyes because it had been years since I was able to bend over and actually get myself off the floor in that position. I was able to try it because my new Journey Family made me feel so comfortable." She remembers all the Journey coaches telling her that they knew she could do it.

In the end, it was all about belief. Mary believed in God and because she believed God, she believed she could do anything with His help. She also believed in her coaches and in return, her coaches believed in her. Today Mary is down 95 pounds. She has renewed energy and confidence. Most importantly, she loves herself again.

TAKE A JOURNEY

Nothing great was ever accomplished without first believing it was possible. Albert Einstein said "Anything imaginable is possible." If right now you are struggling to believe in yourself enough to accomplish your goals then maybe you can try believing in God to strengthen you or maybe you can believe in Journey Fitness to help you. "Faith is the substance of things hoped for, the evidence of things not yet seen." - Hebrews 11:1 Let Mary and others like her be your evidence to have faith and trust the process.

Persistence Pays Off

by Logan Peters

"A river cuts through a rock not because of its power but its persistence."

– James N. Watkins.

Have you ever put your own goals on hold due to "life" getting in the way? For Cathy, this was the case. In the middle of a job change Cathy found herself eating a little more than she typically did. Stress got the best of her in this transition. She felt her eating was in control of her rather than the other way around. Cathy wanted something better for herself. Far too often people get stuck in their routines and life just seems to slip away from them, letting their goals fall to the back burner to be all but forgotten. In Cathy's situation, she was holding on tight to those goals. All she wanted was to be comfortable with who she was. With the stress of her new job and recent weight gain, everything physically was spiraling out of control.

The irony in Cathy's situation was that she had been working out regularly during all of this. That's right, exercise was a regular part of her daily life. But, she was still gaining weight due to stress of the new job. Eventually she signed up with a personal trainer in hopes of improving her routine. Cathy was diligent at following the routine, making sure she did both cardio and resistance training. Still, the results Cathy wanted were not happening. Nor did she feel any more comfortable in her own skin. You can imagine the frustration Cathy experienced.

One day, Cathy heard about this place, Journey Fitness, where a few of her friends had had great success. This got her attention. Like some, the price made Cathy a little nervous and she decided to not join. She stuck with the routine that continued to produce what she called "mediocre" results, leaving her feeling no better than when she started. Finally, something amazing happened for Cathy. Journey Fitness came to her workplace and offered a challenge for their company. She was excited to try it!

From day one Cathy experienced things she hadn't in a long time. Her muscles were sore and she loved it! Cathy was immediately hooked. After the challenge ended Cathy couldn't imagine not continuing. Price no longer became a concern because it was giving her the results she wanted for so long. It's true what they say, you can't put a price on happiness, let alone put a price on your own health and wellness. In Cathy's case, it was about finding what worked for her. She came from a place where she tried it all. Cathy, having two C-sections, had even given up on ever having her abs show again. Guess what? To her surprise she now sees her abs a year after starting. She's also running 5k races, something she has always wanted to do.

Cathy has learned that through hard work and determination, anything is possible. She now feels good in her own body and feels proud of herself. On top of it all, she knows her new healthy lifestyle is setting a great example for her family. Cathy went from feeling out of control to now feeling in total control of her own body.

TAKE A JOURNEY

Never settle. With hard work and focus you can achieve your goals. Even when you're tired and sore, or if you feel you've tried everything you can, you have to keep going. Persistence pays off.

FAITH

By Nicole Wilber

"Let me tell you something you already know.
The world ain't all sunshine and rainbows.
It's a very mean and nasty place. And I don't care
how tough you are. It will beat you to your knees
and keep you permanently there if you let it."

– Rocky Balboa

December 2013 was the first that Kathy walked through the doors at Journey Fitness. She recalls feeling self-conscious about her body and uncomfortable with her appearance. She was looking for overall change. It was very difficult for Kathy to look around the classes and see others who seemed to be so physically fit and confident with their bodies.

As weeks and months went by, Kathy began seeing herself differently. The weight began to drop off and she could feel her strength and stamina improving. She began getting more and more compliments. She was feeling much more comfortable in her clothing and in her own skin. "Half way through my weight loss Journey, I endured the hardest trial in my life. My wonderful husband went home to be with the Lord. There would be days I didn't even want to think about getting up early to workout." This is one time that Travis and Cyndy were most encouraging to Kathy. They encouraged her to stay on the path to reach her fitness goals. Their kind spirit, positive energy and undying faith in Kathy's ability kept her motivation strong. Though some days it was a struggle for Kathy to get to her 4:30 am workout, she continued on with her commitment. Soon, it became an everyday thing. Kathy began to feed off of the positive energy. Though her heart will never fully heal, Kathy found peace by beginning each morning with such encouraging, positive people at Journey Fitness. The connections she made and the strength and encouragement she surrounded herself with helped to heal her broken spirit; it truly saved her.

Now, at 65 years old, Kathy is feeling stronger, both mentally and physically, than she ever has before. Kathy is grateful for her Journey Fitness family and how it has helped her throughout trying times in her life.

TAKE A JOURNEY

Always keep your faith. Who you surround yourself with, you will become. Through trying times, believe in your strength and your faith. Surround yourself with positivity and encouragement; let it lift you, let it save you.

MAKE YOURSELF A PRIORITY

By Logan Peters

"Your life does not get better by chance
it gets better by change."

– Jim Rohn

Have you ever experienced a moment in your life that made you realize it was time to make a change? The year 2010 was one that Karen would never forget. In a short period of time that year, Karen lost six family members to many different health related issues. This unfortunate series of events led her to look at her own health. Karen realized that she had to make a change for the better or her life choices could lead to an early end. It wasn't easy for Karen.

Over the next two years she tried many popular diets and routines but nothing seemed to work. In 2012 Karen found herself at her heaviest weight of 326 pounds when she decided to go for bariatric surgery. With great success at first, Karen experienced 100 pounds of weight loss. Like the other things she tried before, this wasn't sustained for long. She soon found her weight increasing again and gained over 60 pounds back.

You can imagine for Karen that she was physically and emotionally beat down. She was not motivated and everything in life seemed to be a struggle. This was the hardest for Karen because she had always been thin up to the end of college. Then her new sedentary lifestyle led to where she was now. On top of it all, Karen was one to put everyone else's needs before hers. Her health had declined.

Scared by the recent deaths in her family Karen finally worked up the courage to walk through the doors of Journey Fitness. It was hard for Karen, at first, but something told her she was in a good place. She even found that putting herself first was getting easier as she started the program. She scheduled her plans with her friends around her workouts. Then Karen amazed herself. She found herself enjoying her 7am workouts in the morning. Each day, with each workout, Karen continued to work harder and changed the way she approached her nutrition. This allowed her to work towards the 100 lbs. she lost with the surgery. The best part is she now has the tools to make good choices to keep that weight off.

Karen has gone from barely being able to walk through the doors, to driving everyone around her "a little crazy," as she would say, with her continued talk of her new love of fitness and healthy eating habits. Karen now feels in control of her life and is enjoying every moment of it. Karen will be the first to tell you, "Life is too short not to focus on a healthy way of living."

Take a Journey

If you want to make the change you have to be willing to make yourself a priority!

SELF-LOVE IS THE BEST LOVE.

By Ambir Case

"When I didn't like what I saw in the mirror
I decided to change what the mirror would see."

– Ambir Case

Growing up very active and involved in sports her whole life, Toni played softball and basketball from 5 years old until she had children. Toni is a proud mother. Her kids are her world. After having her children and being in a marriage that had a negative impact on her both mentally and emotionally, Toni found she had let go of the active life style she once lived.

Toni wasn't happy and because of this, the unhappiness began to affect all areas of her life until it began to spread outward as well. Toni knew she wasn't comfortable in her skin. She was unable to do even one push-up and was breathless going up the stairs. Her cholesterol and blood pressure were at their worst. What happened to the woman who once excelled in anything physical?

After having children and going through the trials that life brought, Toni found herself looking into the mirror and not loving the person looking back at her. Who was that person? In that moment and throughout that day questions flooded Toni's mind. Who would be there for her children and her grandchildren? She needed to be. This was her turning point, the point of realization that something needed to change. This is when she chose to overcome her fears of working out in front of others, when Toni chose to love and take care of herself again. It is where she found Journey Fitness.

Journey Fitness became Toni's safe haven, where she could walk out better both physically and mentally than when she walked in. Toni has created relationships that make her want to do and be better and never look back.

When I look at Toni, I see a strong and beautiful woman who is an inspiration. Toni is a woman whose story is that of a person, a real person, a mother. Rather than looking in the mirror and giving up, thinking about all of life's stressors playing against her, Toni decided to get better. She didn't want, nor did she have to accept the impostor staring at her in the mirror. She decided that the Toni she used to look at in the mirror was the perfect one. She fought for herself and got Toni back.

TAKE A JOURNEY

We don't have to use life, parenthood, hardships as excuses. Instead use them as motivation to be better because you are worth it.

FEEL BETTER

CHANGE IS AN INSIDE JOB

By Travis Barnes

"Today, you've got a decision to make.
You're gonna get better or you're gonna get worse,
but you're not gonna stay the same. Which will it be?"

– Joe Paterno

Robin Sharma tells a story in his book, "The Monk Who Sold His Ferrari," about a man who came home to his son full of energy and wanting to play, but the father was so tired that all he wanted to do was sit in his chair, read the paper and rest. The son continued to bother the father to play and in an attempt to entertain the son, the father took a page of the paper that had the globe on it and tore it up, challenging the son to see how fast he could put it back together. The father had hoped this project would take a while but when the son returned in just minutes the father was amazed at how fast he had put the globe back together.

The father asked the son "How did you do it?"

The son replied "It was easy. On the other side was a person, and when I put the person back together the world came back together."

And so it goes with helping people. To help someone else, first you must help yourself.

When I think of this story, I think of Dr. Chris Fucito and Dr. Heidi Hodder because of the way they have helped themselves in order to better help the world. They are husband and wife. Heidi was an athlete in school. When she turned 40 she became self-conscious knowing that she needed to lose weight. She said "When you are an ex-athlete and doctor, it is depressing and unacceptable to be overweight."

Journey Fitness appealed to Dr. Hodder because of the team and family-like atmosphere. She was able to learn exercises and modifications that she could pass on to her patients. When her patients would say, "Dr. Hodder, I am too old to lose weight," she would share the stories of people who were over 70 years old getting in shape, losing weight and hanging from pull up bars at Journey Fitness.

There is a quote that says, "A leader of one or a leader of many, if you can't lead one, you can't lead any." (Author Unknown.) And so that story goes with Dr. Hodder, who not only led herself and her patients into positive life change, but also led her mother, Connie Hodder, to Journey Fitness. Heidi reports that her mother now looks younger, is stronger and has better balance than ever before.

"I am very proud of her 'on the toes' push-ups and when she gets up on the pull up bar," she adds.

Six months after Dr. Hodder joined, her husband, Dr. Fucito joined as well. When I asked Dr. Fucito why he joined, he said "To accept new challenges. To push myself in ways I had not done before. To learn new techniques and concepts, to be an inspiration to and better counsel my patients on health and fitness. Also, I hope to inspire the people around me at Journey as well as draw inspiration from them."

How awesome is that? Don't you wish every doctor was like these two investing in their own health so they can better counsel their patients? When you heard that story did it make you think about how many lives Dr. Hodder touched with her one decision to change her health for the better? She changed the life of her patients, which extended to her patient's family, then her mother, and her husband who then helped his patients and their families.

Dr. Chris Fucito and Dr. Heidi Hodder

TAKE A JOURNEY

Never believe that the decisions you are making are only affecting yourself. Stop and think. Who is your healthy lifestyle influencing and who else is counting on your fitness besides you?

YOU JUST NEED TO CHOOSE A DIFFERENT PATH

By Nicole Wilber

"When you come to the end of your rope,
tie a knot and hang on."

– Franklin D Roosevelt

"Not a day goes by that I don't think of Josh. It's been 7 years now. It hasn't gotten any easier."

Robin knows she will never fully accept the death of her son, Josh. You cannot simply 'get over' a loss. You just learn to deal, and hopefully over time, cope with it. Though Robin has lost such a huge part of her life, since then she has gained so much.

Over time, Robin has gained so much support, motivation, and strength. These did not come over night, however. Robin recalls a time when she was at the lowest of low points. It was as though she was reluctantly going through the motions of every day life. No emotion. No desire. Numb. She would drag her feet throughout the workday, only to come home and sit on her couch with a bottle of wine and bag of chips. There was a time she felt so overwhelmed with devastation that she could not imagine living another day, nor did she even want to.

One day all of that changed. Knowing how hopeless Robin felt, her hairdresser, Linda Noble, made a suggestion. She suggested Robin look into a place called Journey Fitness. Robin, now at her heaviest weight, figured she had nothing to lose, so why not?

Immediately, something clicked. She realized that the person she currently was, is not who Josh would want her to be. Josh left behind his beautiful baby girl, Leigha, who was just beginning to walk and run. Robin knew something was going to have to change. Josh would not want her to sit around and cry for the rest of her life. Instead, he would want her to be able to run and play with Leigha. Robin had a newfound motivation for change. She had a responsibility to keep her son's spirit alive, and share that spirit with her granddaughter as much as she could.

Though she is not yet at her goal weight, she is well on her way. Throughout her Journey so far, Robin has gained a new outlook. She has motivation to continue living her healthier lifestyle. She has gained friends that have become family. She has gained confidence and so much strength, mentally and physically. She has learned to be strong for Leigha.

Take a Journey

Family is one of life's greatest blessings. Cherish every second you have with your family, always make time for them. In any instant, your entire world can come crashing down on you to the point you feel that weight is unbearable. Hold on. The old cliché says, everything happens for a reason. You may not agree with it. You may not know what that reason is and you may never find out. You cannot go back in time and you cannot change the past. When you feel that weight is too much to bear, you look life square in the face and tell yourself, the longer you hold on, the stronger that weight makes you. One day at a time.

FIGHT. BELIEVE. HOPE.

By Jeff Case

"I believe everyone needs a coach in life,
and that's what I set out to be every single day."

— JC

**Have you ever known someone who pushes you away
every time you put out a gentle hand?**

In March 2016, The Hilliard Corporation teamed up with
a local fitness center, Journey Fitness (JF). Muriel knew
nothing about Journey Fitness or fitness for that matter. She
loved to walk, but any other exercise was of no interest to her.
Joining a gym had crossed her mind at times, but that was way
out of her comfort zone, so she never even tried. Muriel was
adamant about not joining Journey Fitness or even "liking it" for
that matter. Even so, she somehow managed to give it a try. After
her first day, she could barely walk, but came back day after day.
She also felt no desire to follow the nutritional guidelines of the

Journey Fitness program, and found that even though she was not following the diet, she loved the exercise. I could tell that Muriel loved getting stronger and although still overweight, she loved this process that began to help her get into better shape. Muriel would dabble with the diet and lose a few pounds, but nothing to get really excited about.

In June of 2016, Muriel found out that she needed to have a hysterectomy and decided to set a goal to lose 25 pounds before surgery. Her anxiety was through the roof. So, she went to her coach, JC- Director of the Hilliard location, to lay out her goal and ask for accountability. "He was beyond supportive. He cared about me. He encouraged me. He pushed me. He had faith in me, and found strength in me I never knew I had. He coached me to meet that goal, and it was a huge accomplishment!"

On June 24, 2016, Muriel underwent hysterectomy surgery in Rochester, NY. Her surgery went very well and she was really feeling upbeat about it. However, she was very anxious to get home to her best friend, Tucker-Dane, her dog. Muriel and her sister Kelly were anxiously awaiting the release papers when into her recovery room walks JC and his whole family. Her jaw dropped. She was completely floored. He and his family drove over two hours on his day off to come visit her in the hospital. She said, "This act of kindness really made me feel like someone truly cared about me."

Post-surgery, Muriel couldn't work out for six weeks. JC modified the exercises for her and still does to this day. The coaches at JF show you how to do each exercise and show you modifications. Muriel says, "When you think you've hit your limit and when you think you're finished, it's not over yet."

She was now ready to set another goal for 25 pounds, by October 2016. She crushed that goal too. Now she is down 50 pounds and off her acid reflux pills. She says that she looks and feels better than she has in years. She had lost weight before, but to her, losing the weight with the Journey Fitness exercise plan made her look better. Muriel claims to not be the one to spend money on herself, but she knows that she is worth the investment. She has realized that it's a commitment that she needs in her life and even if she struggles with her diet a bit, she is committed to the exercise program.

Muriel firmly believes that none of this would have been possible for her without the caring heart of JC as her coach and very good friend. She says, "There were times I was planning on not going to the gym because of one reason or another and he would call me and convince me that I was just coming up with excuses to not make it! JC has been my cheerleader the entire time. He is my friend when I really need him. He cared about me when I didn't care about myself and he is so passionate about people."

Muriel says that, "Some folks really like the motivational stories read at the cool down. For some it's the frozen towel after the workout. For me it's the caring coach that made me feel special and loved."

Muriel Parrotte and her trainer, JC

TAKE A JOURNEY

Sometimes we need people in our lives who care more about us than we do. Do you have someone in your life who cares about how you're doing? Sometimes God sends us just what we need when we are feeling out of control. Be a friend to someone today. Share your light, because it may just be the words you speak into some one else's life that saves them.

TAKE CONTROL OF YOU

by Logan Peters

"Taking control of your own creation,
you can ultimately affect your future."

– Dee Wallace

"Is this a dream?" Amanda asked herself as the doctor stepped out of the room. She now sat in complete despair. In one defining moment her world came crashing down. The doctor had just told her that she would never be able to have children. He called it Polycystic Ovarian Syndrome. Along with a list of other side effects, infertility was the one that struck home the hardest. Any dreams of conceiving like a normal woman and having a family of her own were now gone. From there, life only seemed to go downhill.

The next couple of years brought Amanda to her heaviest weight of 220 pounds. She was at risk for diabetes, and was disgusted with the way she looked and felt. On top of it all Amanda chose to leave her husband, after being with him for 12 years, due to his drug abuse which would later claim his young life. Depression was a common experience of everyday life. She even began to pick up more hours at both of her jobs just so she didn't have to be home. This was rock bottom. She was totally defeated and ready to give up.

Fortunately, there was a light at the end of the tunnel. Because she was afraid of having to poke herself with needles testing blood sugars for the rest of her life, she began walking on a treadmill and using an elliptical. Then a friend reached out with a simple invite to Journey Fitness. Little did she know that this one invite would lead her to a life changing experience.

When life seems darkest, leaving us defeated and unhappy, we must reflect inward to determine how we respond. Starting with what we best have control over - ourselves. This was the case for Amanda. In her situation giving up would have been easy. Yet, she knew deep down inside, change was the only way out of her current situation.

Heraclitus said in his writings "All things come into being through opposition and all are in flux like a river." Amanda chose not to fight anymore with the things she could not change and focus in on what she could change. Rather than trying to fight change, she decided to go with the flow of her life. This decision brought light into her new and improved life.

Amanda finally found something that worked for her. She changed her nutrition, adding in exercise, and finding a supportive place to do all of this. Amanda now finds herself far from rock bottom in a place where happiness and joy are more common than sadness. No longer does she live in fear of diabetes and now feels good in her own body. Living by her new mantra, *live, laugh and love*, she will be the first to tell you to love yourself for who you are. You should take care of the person in the mirror. Today is the day to make the change. Don't waste time thinking you can't because you can and you will.

Take a Journey

Don't let things you can't control dictate who you are going to be. Go with the flow and live, laugh and love.

Putting Me First

by Jeremy Purifoy and Linda Fero

"From the concrete
who knew a flower would grow?"

– Drake

Linda Fero and Family - BEFORE

This is not for me! What am I doing? I absolutely hate exercising! But it is only six weeks and my daughter needs my support. I broke it down to myself - three sessions a week, for six weeks is only 18 hours until I am done! As I walk through the doors of Journey Fitness, my expectations are extremely low. I do not consider myself a person who enjoys exercising, not to mention I hate to sweat. During my initial intake with Cyndy, I remember her asking me what goal I would like to accomplish. My response was pretty simple and straight forward - "to lose a size." Cyndy clearly had bigger aspirations for me and it showed on her face, however, her reaction did not do anything for me. I was sticking to my attitude, convinced that I was not going to last beyond the six weeks. I consider myself as a mom first and my daughter asked me to support her. I had mentally committed to 18 visits, three visits per week for 6 bloody weeks! Believe me, I was counting down after every visit to the gym.

There is no denying I was interested in taking some weight off. My entire thought process was to do it like I have done it in the past. Starve myself or deprive myself for a while so that I could get back to eating whatever I want until the next time that I would starve myself. My weight had been a struggle for me my entire life. When I was younger, I was super skinny and teased for it. Then in my early adult years my weight began to accumulate around my hips and thighs. When I started having children, the battle really kicked into high gear resulting in spending more than 25 years overweight. As weight kept adding on, my activity levels slowly became non-existent. In early 2004, I developed a back issue that was not diagnosed until early 2008. For four years I was unable to stand, sit or lie down for an extended amount of time without unbearable pain and discomfort. My activity level declined even more until the doctor finally discovered the problem, performed surgery and gave me my life back! However, by this time I felt like it was too late. I was 285 lbs.! I remember one specific occasion when I was eating and thinking to myself, "What are you doing? You are stuffed yet you continue to eat simply because it tastes good!"

As I approached my 18th visit, I started to come to a cross road on whether I should join or not. I had adopted the low-carb lifestyle and begun to see and feel the benefits of my efforts. I came to the realization if I were to quit now the last six weeks would amount to a waste of time. Therefore, I decided to commit to three more months. I wanted to prove to myself that this whole "exercise thing" was really working for me. Once I began to develop a relationship with the coaches, I began to feel a little differently about going to the gym. I can't speak enough about the impact that every single coach has had on me. Jeremy, and his genuine interest and involvement in my growth and success. Eugene, and his ability to turn ANY negative comment into a positive point of view. Cameron, and his unyielding energy. Zach, and his empathetic, comforting encouragement when an energetic high five isn't what I need. Courtney, and her interest in encouraging me to push beyond my perceived limits. Every single coach has a hand in my continued commitment to myself and this program.

As my three-month membership neared the end, I was gaining confidence in my workouts, seeing the benefits of my efforts and beginning to believe. Any time I began to think, "Maybe I'll skip the gym today," I made myself get dressed and go! My motto had become "get out of your head and into the gym." I was changing mentally as well as physically. After a lifetime of treating my weight as a thing that is either addressed or ignored, I had begun to realize that my weight is not a temporary thing. It is not something that I will either be gaining or losing. I have begun to see that my weight is something I can manage. Now I see it as a lifelong commitment to myself, instead of seeing an exercise program or the next best diet as a temporary fix to get me to the point where I can return to crappy eating habits and laziness. I see myself as someone who exercises and makes better food choices as a habit that I will carry into my later years. My children, husband and friends were so encouraging and supportive once they saw how successful this program was for me. I decided to join for a year "just to see what will happen." Over the next 3 or 4 months, my commitment really kicked in.

I'm at the 6-month mark and I have lost 45 pounds and dropped three sizes! I am feeling great! My energy has sky rocketed to the point where I have become a more productive person and feel less overwhelmed by my daily responsibilities. My sleep habits improved as well as my confidence. I have become a more positive person who encourages and roots for those individuals who are embarking on their own Journey. Perhaps most surprising to me is how people come to me for advice and encouragement. I am happy to impart any wisdom I may have acquired along the way but the very idea that I am considered "fit" is still new to me.

Today, I am fully invested and cannot see myself not exercising. I make good food choices most of the time, and I am okay with that. I belong to a community of people here at Journey Fitness who strive not for perfection, but for improvements, and there is always room for that!

In the end, it is Jeremy who summed it up so well for me. I am proof that a flower really can grow from concrete!

TAKE A JOURNEY

Train your mind to see the good in all situations! A positive mindset will lead to positive results.

DETERMINATION

By Travis Barnes

"Never, Never, Never Give Up"

– Winston Churchill

Have you ever felt like quitting? I think we all have. Now when I think of quitting I think of this poem and Linda Noble who has taught me what it means to *never give up*. Here is the famous poem, "***Don't Quit***," by John Greenleaf Whittier.

> When things go wrong, as they sometimes will,
> When the road you're trudging seems all up hill,
> When the funds are low and the debts are high
> And you want to smile, but you have to sigh,
> When care is pressing you down a bit,
> Rest if you must, but don't you quit.
> Life is strange with its twists and turns
> As every one of us sometimes learns
> And many a failure comes about
> When he might have won had he stuck it out;
> Don't give up though the pace seems slow—

You may succeed with another blow.
Success is failure turned inside out—
The silver tint of the clouds of doubt,
And you never can tell just how close you are,
It may be near when it seems so far;
So stick to the fight when you're hardest hit—
It's when things seem worst that you must not quit.

Linda was only 23 years old when her mother passed away from breast cancer at the age of 42. She always feared she might suffer the same fate and then on a cold January morning in 2012, she was diagnosed with Stage 3 breast cancer. In the following months, she was subjected to 16 rounds of chemotherapy followed by a double mastectomy and reconstructive surgery. Unfortunately, the cancer resisted the treatment so she required 8 more surgeries before the cancer was removed. Did chemotherapy make her sick? You bet it did. Did she ever feel like the surgeries weren't working? Of course she did. Still Linda knew there was only one path to beat her cancer, and she was determined to win. It was an uphill battle and she stuck it out.

After 16 rounds of chemo and 9 surgeries her body was run down but she was cancer free. If she did nothing but live a sedentary life after that, no one would have blamed Linda but the amazing thing about winning is that it becomes a habit.

In the words of the famous coach, Vince Lombardi, "Winning is not a sometime thing; it's an all the time thing. You don't win once in a while... you don't do things right once in a while... you do them right all the time. Winning is habit."

Linda was grateful for her victory over cancer but her battle was not over because beating cancer was just part of reclaiming her health. Instead of another dose of drugs she was ready for a daily dose of exercise. She wanted to have her strength and energy back. She was investigating fitness opportunities when her friend, Diane Mastrantonio, told her about Journey Fitness. Linda decided to give it a try. She found the workouts to be challenging especially after her recent battle with cancer, but Linda learned something else about winning when she joined Journey Fitness. She learned, that if you want to win, then you need to put yourself in a winning environment. Linda defines a winning environment as one of support, motivation, dedication and love. She says, "that is what I found at Journey Fitness." Before coming here, Linda had not belonged to a gym for more than a few months but 4 years later she is still winning her battles at Journey Fitness. Thank you, Linda, for joining Journey Fitness and for teaching us all what it means to *never give up.*

Linda Noble

Take a Journey

Never Quit. Never Give Up. Create that mindset. Then make it a habit. And when you put yourself in a winning environment then you will find success.

ONE BATTLE AT A TIME

By Wendy Lupo

"Nothing tastes as good as healthy feels."

– Author Unknown

Dave Holleran - Before

Training along-side Dave, early one spring morning, I was curious. I turned to him and asked, "Why did you initially decide to be a part of our Waverly Schools Fitness Challenge? What was your motivation?"

His quick response was, "To win the money of course."

At the time I asked, Dave was close to his goal of one hundred pounds lost by the end of June. I had to question if that was the real reason he joined the challenge that January day. In the end, he didn't walk away with the first-place prize, but something much more valuable. Let me tell you his story.

Dave was hired to work for the Waverly District in September of 2012. Elmira laid off teachers the year before which brought Dave to the Waverly Middle School. My daughter actually had Dave as her social studies teacher his first year here. I remember because she came home extremely upset one day telling me that her teacher had cancer.

Initially the doctors thought he had a cyst on the back of his neck. There was no reason to believe that the tests would come back as a malignant lymph node. Dave was originally diagnosed with Ewing Sarcoma, a very aggressive cancer usually found in children. After visiting specialists at the University of Pittsburgh Medical Center and Roswell Park Cancer Center, it was determined that Dave was misdiagnosed by local doctors and had Angiomatoid Fibrous Histiocytoma. This meant no chemotherapy, just a resection to widen the margins of the original lymph node removal site. One month before, Dave had learned that he was going to be a father. While Dave had some relief that he would be here to raise his unborn child, he continued to struggle with the fear of recurrence. This constant fear led to an unhealthy lifestyle. In Dave's words,

122

he was obese, constantly fatigued, lacked confidence, and had a slight case of hypochondria. At one point in his recovery, Dave's therapist diagnosed him with PTSD. He was short fused and angry at the person he had become. He was anti-social and constantly starting things that he did not finish. This was not Dave. He was suffering and so was his family.

So, the reasons for joining the challenge? His family - his wife, Gigi, and his daughter, Amelia. He didn't want his little girl to have a dad that couldn't play with her. He also wanted his wife to have a better husband. They had both been through so much. It was time to make things better - the way they should be. And finally, the scale! When the scale reads 361.8, Dave says, "You are closer to 400 than 300!" He was a college athlete, and wanted to get back to a healthy lifestyle.

After losing the weight that he did during the initial fitness challenge, Dave became motivated to lose more. The Journey program and message really clicked with him. He met some really "good" people which made it easier to stay with Journey even after his teammates from the challenge decided not to stay on as members. The comradery resonated with Dave and the workouts challenged him. The tools Dave has adopted are invaluable to him. The dietary tips, motivational text messages, the coaching, along with the support of his wife (not only emotionally, but helping with food prep) have all been beneficial to his success.

After the loss of 100 pounds and completing his first 5k, Dave cannot imagine going back to his old life style.

Dave Holleran - After

TAKE A JOURNEY

When the task seems too huge, too insurmountable, too enormous to tackle, take one day at a time, one battle at a time, anything is possible. "Just keep moving forward, one day at a time. The view from the top is SO worth the climb."

I AIN'T QUITTIN'!

By Jeff Case

*"Today ain't that day, and
it doesn't look pretty for tomorrow either."*

– Martin Rooney

Joe Horton was 10 minutes into his first Journey Fitness Workout when he couldn't breathe. He ran for his inhaler and as he took a deep breath he struggled to find oxygen. It was in this moment that Joe thought to himself, this is bullshit. "I don't need to do this stuff just to feel like crap." It was in that moment, that first 10 minutes, that Joe was faced with a choice - a choice all too familiar for many of us here today. Do I want to be a quitter? That's where Joe Horton was when he made his choice.

Joe said, "I aint quittin!"

I shared with Joe something I heard from Martin Rooney, and that was, "Today ain't that day, and it doesn't look pretty for tomorrow either."

Joe knew how out of shape he was. But the old Joe wouldn't do anything about it. He just found it easier to not deal with it. Joe said that he wouldn't exert himself to do anything where he would lose his breath. You can imagine how uncomfortable this was for him. He had to endure his workout running for the inhaler every 10 minutes. Joe was also dealing with back and knee issues as he was carrying extra weight up top. Every pound is an extra four pounds on the joints and Joe was feeling it. Just climbing the stairs at work would take his breath away. Sometimes we don't even realize how all the little choices over time accumulate to the big unhealthy picture.

Can you relate to Joe? Do you find yourself getting frustrated with your kids, spouse, friends, and relationships because you're not in control of your health?

Joe was experiencing this. He would find himself becoming frustrated with his granddaughters, whom he loves so deeply, simply because he was out of shape and feeling sick, thick and tired. He just found it really hard to keep up with them.

More importantly, however, there was Joe Horton, the loving man and grandpa. He could stay the same or just decide to be better. Joe's attitude took a quick shift in that defining moment where he made the choice to be better. His attitude became stronger. He began to understand that what he was putting himself through was all about him. He came to realize that he is worth it and he knew that he could be better - better for his granddaughters, six-year-old Zoe and 13-year-old Sarah.

You see? That's what it's all about ladies and gentlemen - finding your WHY? Take back control of your life. I always say, "The stronger you are, the better you will be for you, your family and your relationships."

Joe is down over 40 pounds, looking for slimmer clothes and is going on our Journey Fitness Wall of Fame. What kept Joe in the game? It wasn't just that defining moment when he couldn't breathe his first day. Joe has found other value on his Journey that keeps him going further and further. It's the constant support and encouragement from not only his coaches, but his workout buddies too. Joe can see the results of his hard work paying off. He has found nutrition to be very crucial in his success. He said the nutrition is what had him feeling better. The workouts on the other hand? They are tough.

Joe reminds himself daily that this time he spends at Journey Fitness is for him. When he's having a tough workout, you can hear him say, "This is all about me! Today ain't that day. I ain't quittin!"

JC and Joe Horton

TAKE A JOURNEY

"You have to make a choice. The days can either add up for you or against you? You decide."

— Jeff Case (JC)

BETTER TOGETHER

By Jeremy Purifoy

"It's always better when we're together."

– Jack Johnson

Bruce and Penny Schoonover

It was time for a change! Penny and Bruce Schoonover surrounded themselves with people who were making differences in their own personal life. Many of their friends were making progress with weight loss, feeling better, looking better and some were discontinuing their medications. In late December 2014, Penny and Bruce took a 20-minute drive to Elmira, New York to begin a new Journey to a new beginning. A friend of Bruce's had lost a large amount of weight which made the Schoonover's even more motivated and curious about how their friend was dropping all this weight. Later they learned that their friend was a member at Journey Fitness and loved making his workouts. Once informed about how he was making this transformation Bruce became all about Journey Fitness. He delivered his friend's feedback to Penny, and she knew that she had to get to Journey Fitness *fast*.

Penny and Bruce attended an Open House at Journey Fitness Elmira that was scheduled right before the New Year. This Open House was all that the Schoonover's needed to convince themselves that Journey Fitness is what they needed. Another important selling point, Journey Fitness was expanding to Corning which was an easier commute. Although this was huge, they knew this program was going to be perfect and what they needed to be successful. Penny states, "Two and a half years later it is still exactly what we needed."

Before Journey Fitness, Bruce had two goals. The first was to lose weight and the second was to build muscle. Bruce is over sixty, so he felt a bit intimidated. After about three weeks, he began to see that reaching his goals was do-able! He often talks about how he cannot get enough of the coaching at Journey. The coaches at Journey Fitness play a pivotal part in Bruce's success. Being over 60 years of age, Bruce would never have thought he could accomplish the amount he has done. Bruce did not one, but two Spartan races in the same year!

Bruce was Journey Fitness Corning's first Wall of Famer. Our Wall of Fame is for the members who achieve their long-term goal. Just before joining Journey Fitness, Bruce was at 240 lbs. and he was a Type 2 diabetic. His health could no longer be taken for granted. He started losing weight by cutting back on what he was eating but that was not enough. He needed to workout. All  he had to do was show up and believe me, after the workouts he was definitely feeling the burn. Also, Bruce now has a better understanding of good nutrition and what works best for his body or does not react well. In Bruce's first 6 months he dropped 25 lbs. and started to build muscle mass. Now on the golf course he feels so much stronger. He can even squat when lining up a putt instead of getting down on one knee!

Prior to Penny's Journey she was at a point in her life that she knew it was time to do something. She had not exercised in years. Her weight had reached a point that she seriously wondered if she would ever be able to lose it. Penny was frustrated and embarrassed of her own size. She hated worrying about what Bruce thought about her appearance.

Penny's tipping point was when she refused to buy the next size larger in clothes! Nine months have passed in their Journey. During these 9 months, Bruce and Penny went to Scotland on a 100-mile hiking vacation. It was an experience like no other. These mountains were not small peaks, and they both agreed that if it had not been for their preparation at Journey Fitness prior to the trip, that they would not have been able to accomplish the hike. They were beyond thankful to have lost several pounds and built up their muscles before they left.

Incorporating a new lifestyle with eating habits made such a huge difference. They changed their diets to a high protein, low carb, and little to no sugar has been key to their success. It really was not that difficult for them to make this adjustment. Bruce and Penny admit that they are far from perfect, but they have a better understanding. Now when they do slip up, they are able to jump back on to the wagon and get the results that they want to see at a faster pace. Cheat meals are not every day meals.

Note from Penny: *"As cliché as it might sound, our coaches make the workouts fun with such high energy. I cannot say enough about them and the superb trainers that they are! They are a huge part of our success! We have also made some amazing new friends at Journey! We have become accountability partners for each other and keep building each other up! How cool is that?"*

The Journey Fitness family is on a lifetime Journey together! Let's make it a healthy and happy one! Everyone can do it! Life is what you make out of it. Every activity and hobby that you have done for several years will become easier and much more enjoyable to do!

Take a Journey

Get your spouse or a friend to keep you accountable. Together you can accomplish more!

Endless Possibilities

by Jesse King

"I am convinced that life is 10% what happens to me and 90% how I react to it."

– Charles Swindoll

Seven years ago, Kevin Romer made his way down to the track for his evening walk. As he started his second mile he felt this sudden, excruciating chest pain shoot straight through his back.

It was here, in this moment, that 58-year-old Kevin Romer experienced a traumatic cardiac event, and received what he calls one of his many "wake up calls." About a year ago I personally had the opportunity to meet with Kevin for a fitness consultation at Journey Fitness Ithaca. Obviously, Kevin survived the event, and recovered enough physically to meet with me. At our initial meeting, I learned the magnitude of his desire to change. It turned out that Kevin's reason for change had a great deal of emotion behind it, so much that at one point during our conversation it even brought a tear to his eye.

At our first meeting Kevin shared with me that he's married, has four children and one grandson. His mom passed away in January of 2016. One of his last few memories of her was when she was in the hospital. He went to visit her, and during their visit she patted him on my stomach and said, "Man, you're fat." From Kevin's tone of voice as he told the story I could sense that his mother's remarks struck home. But I also got the sense that his mother's remarks were not the only thing that prompted Kevin to meet with me, and they were not the driving force behind his reason for change.

Kevin proceeded, fortified with courage, and shared more of his story. I learned about the heart attack he had 7 years ago, and as a result had a stent inserted. Then two years later Kevin began to experience chest pain again. It turns out he needed a second stent placed. This time for a blockage in the "left anterior descending" (LAD) artery commonly known as the "widow maker".

Ironically, after dodging the "widow maker" Kevin struggled to find the motivation to change his lifestyle. According to Kevin the wake-up calls weren't getting through, and perhaps much of his struggle to change was attributed to coming to grips with the fact that he had a problem. But even despite all the red flags, Kevin still struggled to find a solution to address his health issues.

At one point Kevin thought he may have found a solution. After completing cardiac rehab, he made the appointment for gastric bypass surgery. He needed to get the weight off and his doctors all agreed. The problem was that after gastric bypass surgery you can't eat so much which forces a lifestyle change. Conflicted by his doctor's suggestions Kevin decided against surgery. He wasn't prepared to change his lifestyle.

So here we were, sitting and talking several years after his last cardiac event and Kevin still needed to get the weight off. It was at this moment where I learned Kevin's "why" for coming to Journey Fitness. It's what he called 'his real goal.' With a tear in his eye Kevin described a recent doctor visit. His doctor referenced the BMI chart. His BMI was at, or near, 47. Kevin's doctor briefly gave him a lecture, and concluded by reminding him that he was morbidly obese. The phrase, "morbidly obese," hit him hard. In that defining moment Kevin made up his mind that the term would be removed from his medical chart. He did not want to die being "morbidly obese."

Since joining Journey Fitness Kevin has worn the 20-pound weight vest for achieving his 20 pounds of weight loss. Kevin is down 65 total pounds (45 at Journey). His BMI has dropped to 38 (now just "obese", but no longer "morbidly obese"). His diabetes is under control with an A1C at 5.8 (from a high of near 10), and most importantly, he is happier than he has been in a long time. Kevin looks forward to hating every session at Journey Fitness and loving every ice-cold towel when we are done. He likes this "love-hate" relationship because it works for him.

TAKE A JOURNEY

Life can seem intense at times. But what's encouraging is the fact that we all possess the power to steer our own course towards either triumph or tragedy. Take the first step today, and start believing in the amazing possibilities for you. Stop suffering from possibility blindness! According to Kevin "It can be done. If I can do it you can do it." Believing in what's possible for you is the first step towards triumphing over your struggles.

ONE MORE ROUND

By Logan Peters

*"Going one more round when you don't think you can.
That's what makes all the difference in your life."*

– Rocky

Have you ever felt as if you just existed in a world that seemingly passed around you? This is how Deanna felt. At 22 years old, she found herself dragging herself out of bed for yet another miserable day at work. She felt that life seemed to be passing by right before her eyes as she trudged through her normal daily activities. She felt tired, weak, depressed and anti-social. Deanna couldn't even force herself to do anything other than get up, go to work and go back home for bed. This had become accepted as a normal daily routine.

Deanna felt that her current way of life was as good as it was going to get. Yet, there was something inside her that just wouldn't settle for the unhappiness. Although the world around her didn't feel all that great, Deanna knew there had to be more to life than her current situation. She wanted to do more than just exist. She wanted to live.

Deanna's feelings began in high school. She was very active in sports and activities. But, she remembers not feeling good in her own body. As her high school career came to an end Deanna started to put on weight which brought her to the heaviest weight she'd ever been. At this point, she needed to make a change.

Then it happened. One day at work, Deanna heard about a 21-day fitness challenge her work was going to participate in with Journey Fitness. This challenge came with a chance to win a cash prize. Now, Deanna was very competitive and felt confident in her ability to win the money - especially if it was only for 21 days. Little did she know her motivation to win some cash would lead her to one of the most positive life changing experiences.

Deanna went on to win the competition and found herself still going 5 months later and about 40 pounds lighter, and sticking with a healthier nutrition. Deanna will tell you this was the only thing she has ever sustained. For her it became about more than just weight loss. Deanna started to notice that after every workout her life seemed to get a little bit better. Day after day she fought for her happiness. Her new-found fitness family and friends kept her motivated and she was now feeling as if she could enjoy life. It was something she had been missing for a long time. It was as if someone flipped on a switch and her world went from bleak to better than ever! Even work became more enjoyable.

Robin Sharma in his book, "The Monk Who Sold His Ferrari," describes how, in certain situations, we must change the world within to change the world around us. That's exactly what Deanna did. Adapting a healthier way of life, Deanna finally found what she was looking for - a Journey that led her to feeling good about herself. It has even come to a point that if she skips a workout she doesn't feel as good as when she does workout.

Take a Journey

The dream will be built on the little victories we win each day in the trenches. When it gets hard or you feel like giving up, push yourself to go "one more round" and you will see your life change right before your eyes.

Trust the Process

By Jeff Case

*"You may see me struggle,
but you will never see me quit."*

– Unknown

Have you ever felt like you were being selfish for taking time for yourself to exercise? And then afterwards, whether it was your own thoughts or maybe someone close to you, made you feel guilty about it? Have you ever felt sad, discouraged, ugly, and out of control? Have you ever felt like you were drowning in life and then someone hands you a piece of cake and tells you not only can you have it but you can eat it too?

That's where Mina Barron was when she was faced with a choice. She refused to buy a size 18 pair of pants. She felt a mess, overweight and only 5 feet 5 inches tall. Her doctor labeled her as obese and prescribed her cholesterol meds.

On top of that, she was feeling depressed, timid, unmotivated, lazy, tired, and unhappy. She suffered from restless leg syndrome, ate fast food a lot, and drank alcohol almost daily. She also drank a lot of really sweet coffee drinks and rarely drank water. Mina remembers feeling angry all the time and disgusted with herself which carried over to the people in in her life that she loved. That's when the opportunity to do something about it came "knocking on her door."

Her husband, Brent, works at the Hilliard Corporation. In March 2016, the company had received a Journey Fitness gift basket that offered them a corporate challenge for their employees. These corporate challenges fall perfectly into the Journey Fitness mission to create impact in as many lives as possible as well as benefits the corporate setting by helping their employees become healthier hence creating a more productive work environment and cuts down on health insurance costs. It's a win for both.

Mina saw this as an opportunity to gain control of her life again, and it was so convenient for her that she couldn't say no.

The most motivating factor was that the health of her parents was declining, and she considered them to be young. It was coupled with the fact that her own children were 14 and 10, Mina was scared that she would be terribly unhealthy and her kids would be stuck caring for her when they were so young. Mina felt that she desperately needed to get her act together!

Have you ever found yourself doing something that was supposed to help you feel better but realized you were doing it just to please someone else?

Mina was a huge "people pleaser," She didn't want to disappoint her coach by gaining weight or eating poorly. She never wanted to see the number on the scale go up! But, after a while, Mina began to change her mind set in a healthier way. Mina began recognizing her Journey as her own and no one else's! She stopped looking at her Journey as a temporary change, but as a new healthy life-style that she can commit to long term. That's how she wants to live.

Mina explains that it is not at all easy! However, it does get easier and is so important and worth all the effort! Mina has a new-found determination! She has a goal of reaching a 50-pound weight loss that she has not yet reached yet, but is a weigh in away from achieving and she will not be giving up! She feels much stronger and healthier and even impresses her 15-year-old daughter, Isabel. "And that is no small feat," she adds.

This is what Mina had to say, "The healthier I am, the more I am able to help those that I care about. I no longer look at eating healthy or exercising as an extravagance or guilt trip. I see it as a necessary and integral part of what makes me, me. Seeing the weight come off and the clothes getting smaller have been huge motivators for me. I work my schedule around getting to work out. I have many more new and wonderful friends that are like minded. I run races now! I don't always like it, but I have the confidence to know that I can do it! This Journey has changed my life for the better! Oh and of course, people noticing my progress has helped as well!"

Mina Barrons Before and After with JC

Take a Journey

Don't rush the process, trust the process!!! In the end, it's the Journey that matters!

PRIDE is an Acronym
(Personal Responsibility In Daily Efforts)

By Wendy Lupo

*"Discipline is choosing between what you want now
and what you want most."*

– Augusta F. Kantra

"You're okay. Settle down. Just breathe. This shall pass," Tina would say to herself. They would come on without notice. When the initial panic attack came on, she thought it must be a heart attack. She felt a lack of being in control of her own body. Her heart raced and she felt alone. She couldn't describe what was going on inside her. When they continued, she was prescribed medicine for the attacks along with her depression. Tina came to believe that medicine was a cure for any aliment, add alcohol to the mix and all was good. Until the day her throat tightened and she had difficulty swallowing.

After many tests, the doctor's response was frank. He stressed to Tina that she must lose weight. She had put on so much weight that her diaphragm was pushing against her stomach and esophagus, causing throat constrictions. She described her experiences of the gagging this caused while eating. The doctor told her that if she did not take action, her next experience could be a prescribed C-Pap machine.

Pressure from the excess weight was also causing symptoms of sleep apnea. Tina thought nothing of putting on weight over the years. Her main focus was to take care of her family, not herself. She was comfortable with her husband of thirty years and knew he would not leave her because she looked "okay". She resolved herself to the fact that she was never going to be small and would just live with it.

Dr. Fuscito's words would change all that. Tina did not want to die at a young age. She did not want to live like this anymore. She needed to do something. Her doctor immediately prescribed Journey Fitness, along with the words, "Tina, you are a strong person. Take charge!"

That very weekend, Tina walked through the doors of the Elmira Journey location not knowing what the other side of that door would hold for her. She was scared as Hell and knew no one. She sat with Michele Kelley, one of the personal trainers. With Michele's upbeat attitude and explanation of the process, Tina knew it would all be okay. She signed up on the spot, intake and all.

Tina was committed! She began prepping food, journaling, and reading labels at the grocery store. She even encouraged her whole family to eat the same way. Tina also cut out alcohol. She was in for life, and she was ready to make a lifestyle change. The weight came off. She enjoyed trainers "wowing" every time she weighed in, and her pants were falling-down around her. The feeling was so intoxicating that she became obsessed.

There was a point about two months into her health Journey that Tina became afraid. She was afraid to cheat, afraid to treat herself. She was afraid that if she ate certain foods, she would put all her weight back on. With the support of the team of trainers and her family, she overcame her fear.

In a year, Tina lost sixty-five pounds. She went from a size sixteen to a size four. "I look in the mirror more than I ever have, even taking selfies," Tina smiles! "I feel great and cannot believe the things I can do."

Journey Fitness has become much more than Tina's fitness center. It is now her place of employment, a place to share her healthy routine with her husband, and her place of CHANGE.

Tina Lockner - Before   Tina Lockner - After

Take a Journey

"You are the only one in control of yourself, TAKE PRIDE!"
Change is an act. "If you do not change direction, you may
end up where you are heading."

– Lao Tau

WHAT ARE YOU RUNNING FROM?

By Jesse King and Carmel Macali

"The fears you run away from run toward you.
The fears you don't own will own you. But
behind every fear wall lives a precious treasure."

– Robin Sharma

I remember feeling lost, anxious, and apprehensive when I first walked into Journey Fitness. I was so scared I wanted to cry!

But I knew I had to do something. I was at a point in life where something needed to change. Walking through the doors of Journey Fitness I lacked self-confidence. I began thinking, "I don't think I can do this." I consoled myself by saying, "Okay, two weeks, I will try it." I never imagined I would go past the two weeks. Remarkably I was shocked at what I could do in just my first workout. I knew by the second workout that I found something that could help change my life.

My weight has been an issue my entire life. I have struggled to lose weight as long as I can remember. Any time I've ever lost weight I would just end up putting back on even more. I was stuck. I was also struggling with knee pain. It hurt everyday just from walking!

My motivation was to get healthier for my family. Being unhealthy scared me. But that changed when I first lost 20lbs. My husband said, "You are so much happier than you used to be. You're the happy Carmel again." That made me smile. When I gained back the weight, I was devastated. However, since joining Journey Fitness I feel like I've found myself again, and my self-confidence.

My life today is great. I have lost over 25 lbs , and I have little to no knee pain. I was due for a shot in my knee for pain in December, and I didn't need it! I was taking Advil all day, but not anymore. I clean a four-story sorority house for a living, and I used to be so out of breath all day cleaning. Now I have so much more energy at work, it's amazing. I used to watch my grandkids play, now I join in. I can't wait for snowmobile season. It's going to be so much fun. I'm looking forward to not feeling so out of breath!

One important lesson I have learned from my experience is to stop putting myself down. I have to stop saying, "Oh I can't do that," or "Oh I can't have that, I am on a diet." Now I am confident with my lifestyle choice, and I'm happy with myself. My mantra is

"I am confident and courageous. I possess the strength and ability to accomplish my goal and dreams!"

Take a Journey

In the words of motivational speaker, Eric Thomas, "Tension produces greatness." In the middle of Carmel's struggles, Carmel found the pain of staying the same was greater than the initial pain she felt while making a change. By finding the courage to try her first workout, and going through the initial pain, the tension in her life eventually subsided. You can do the same, and use pain or fear to your advantage. Start today by shifting your perspective on pain and fear. Use your obstacles as opportunities. Instead of running, or neglecting to address your fears, go towards them. On the other side of pain and fear is a life beyond your wildest dreams.

SELF CONFIDENCE

By Jeff Case

*"You can make excuses or you can make progress,
but you can't do both."*

– Unknown

Do you feel like you're living in self-doubt?

Michele was already living in self-doubt before she ever stepped foot into Journey Fitness. She was planning her excuses for failure even before she started. Does that sound familiar?

Furthermore, she was glad that none of her friends had signed up for Journey Fitness with her. Michele's thought was that if none of her friends signed up then she didn't have to worry about disappointing them when she would eventually quit. However, what Michele didn't count on were all the new friends that she would meet at Journey Fitness who would not "buy" her excuses, and not allow her to quit. And believe me, she tried! Eventually

Michele realized that she did have a friend who signed up for Journey. She would call Michele every time she found out that Michele was thinking about quitting. This friend would keep Michele on the phone until she agreed to give it another chance, and Michele was so glad she did. Have you ever heard the term, friends don't let friends quit the gym? Neither have I. I think I just made it up- but Michele found out that friends don't let friends quit the gym and she would not know where she would be today if this friend hadn't held her accountable. All the new fitness friends, along with the trainers (who have also become friends), helped to keep Michele motivated and hold her accountable, which is exactly what she needed.

Very soon, Michele realized that she can't "diet" her way to a healthier version of herself. She had to make a conscious decision to make this Journey a life-style change. Have you ever heard of the flat-tire story? Michele states, "Don't get me wrong, I fall off the wagon and make horrible choices sometimes, but the key is that I don't stay there and flatten the other three tires. I fix the flat and get back on track making the choices I know I need to make, to get me where I want my Journey to take me."

Everyone is on a Journey to fitness. It's not the destination that matters, but the Journey that gets you there. The question is, "Do you like the destination you're approaching?" Michele had low carb "dieted" on and off for about 15 years. She would sign up for weight loss contests, be extremely strict with her carb intake, drop some pounds in a hurry, and then still lose the contest – *every time*. When the contests were over she would go back to her "normal" way of eating and she always gained back what she had lost, and then some. Does this sound familiar to anyone? This yo-yo lifestyle took Michele to her heaviest point – 248 pounds – in February of 2015. Around that same time some young, energetic gentleman named JC came to the Hilliard Corporation and led their company in a better way, to feel great, and lose weight. Journey Fitness held a 21 Day Weight Loss Challenge contest to kick off Hilliard's introduction to the program, so, of course Michele was in. Have you been really gung-ho about trying a weight-loss program but felt to embarrassed to weigh in with the trainer at your heaviest weight? Well Michele was so much so that she hit the low carb diet life hard for two weeks before she initially weighed in for the contest.

Today Michele is down 50 lbs. and feels much better. Her family has also adopted better habits and is a part of the Journey Fitness family. She loves the support and community that Journey Fitness creates at every single session!

Michele Morgan – Before and After

TAKE A JOURNEY

It's important to have someone who cares enough to hold you accountable to your goals. Whether it's a friend who calls you every time you're thinking about quitting and doesn't get off the phone until you get rid of your "stinkin-thinkin," or your trainer that believes in you more than you do yourself. We really are better together.

LEARN TO LOVE YOURSELF

By Nicole Wilber

"You yourself, as much as anybody in the entire universe, deserve your love and affection."

– Buddha

Leigh Kaminsky

"Natalie didn't ask me to play with her today. This is unusual, she asks me every day." Leigh remembers very distinctly when her daughter Natalie, now 7, stopped asking her to run around the yard with her. She began asking her grandma and grandpa instead, knowing Leigh would turn down Natalie's request. Disappointment. One of the worst feelings there is;

especially when your disappointment is with yourself. How could Leigh let herself become this person whom she was so disappointed with?

All day, the only thing she could think about was going home to sleep. Once she would lie down at night, she could not fall asleep for the life of her. Aside from a backwards sleep cycle, eating take out multiple times a day, Leigh was feeling the effects of a sedentary lifestyle. She hated the way she looked, hated the way she felt. Leigh was incredibly self-conscious, feeling very uncomfortable in her own skin. Those around her suffered as well. Leigh would take her emotions out on those closest to her. That is, if she hadn't already cut them off completely. Leigh's high anxiety did not help the equation.

The one who suffered the most though, was Natalie. She got so used to her mother saying she didn't feel like playing with her, or she wasn't up to it today, that she just stopped asking. This hit Leigh pretty hard; she knew it was time for a change. Enter Journey Fitness.

Leigh, a beautiful young lady with a long, lean build, does not look like your typical Journey Fitness candidate, as most members are focused on significant weight loss. Though she was incredibly nervous to get started, she was determined. When some of her friends got wind that she was starting at Journey, they teased her that it would be too difficult, it wasn't something she could handle. With the nay-sayers, and more importantly, Natalie, in mind, Leigh tenaciously began her Journey.

Two years later, Leigh has lost over 30 pounds. It's not the physical weight though that is the biggest accomplishment for Leigh. It is the weight off her shoulders that she is most proud of. She has gained much more than she has lost. She has gained confidence and happiness. She has gained strength, mentally and physically. She has gained motivation and support. She has gained a new outlook and loves her healthy lifestyle. Leigh is an amazing role model for her daughter. Aside from making healthy choices for them, she engages in positive self-talk and promotes positive self-image for Natalie.

Though everyone thought Leigh's slender frame was beautiful before, it did not help her to feel any more confident in her own skin. If you do not feel comfortable and confident with whom you are, you are not the only one that suffers. Others around you will suffer. Though it may sound cliché, it truly is not about what anybody else thinks. If you do not love yourself first and foremost, how can you possibly love anyone else? You, yourself, deserve your own affection, more than anyone.

TAKE A JOURNEY

Loving yourself is so important. Begin to focus on the positives within yourself. What do you like about yourself? What do you enjoy? Learning to love yourself is an important step in your Journey.

MOVE BETTER

LONG TERM PLEASURE FOR SHORT TERM PAIN

By Travis Barnes

*"Life is not Happening to you.
Life is Responding to you."*

– Rhonda Byrne

What's your goal? What's your fitness dream? Would you like to pass like Jack LaLanne did at the age of 96 reportedly having done a workout the same day? Would you like to live life to the fullest allowing yourself to have the best quality of life? Then the answer is simple. You must be willing to plant seeds so you can harvest later. You will reap what you sow.

When I think of this important life lesson, I think of my friend Dr. Williams. He is 77 years young. He is a retired Navy Captain and a retired Doctor of Radiology. He and his wife, Sherryl, have been married for 50 years. Together they travel the world and take amazing adventures such as African Safaris. Sherryl joined Journey Fitness in 2013 and not long after, Dr. Williams joined to support her Fitness Journey. He soon learned that the Journey Fitness workouts were an excellent compliment to his practice of yoga. Dr. Williams has been practicing yoga for nearly 30 years and while most people his age struggle to get up and down off the floor, he does this task easily. He is able to wrap his feet up around his head and do things that many people half his age cannot do. Dr. Williams has a firm belief that many of the problems he diagnosed as a Radiologist, including things such as falling and breaking a hip, would have been prevented if more people practiced yoga and exercised regularly.

The problem is that most people don't exercise consistently enough to experience the same kind of results as Dr. Williams. Why not? Perhaps it is because the outcomes are invisible. You make a poor choice, and you are rewarded in the moment such as when you eat that piece of chocolate cake. You make a good choice, and you get rewarded later on such as when you achieve the kind of mobility and flexibility enjoyed by Dr. Williams. Life is yin and yang. It is action and reaction. Short-term pain will bring you long-term pleasure but short-term pleasure will bring you long-term pain.

"When we do what is hard, life will be easy. When we do what is easy, life will be hard." – Les Brown

Dr. Williams compares the practice of yoga to the practice of orthodontia. Just like the teeth, the muscles progress a bit each time but the outcome is not immediately visible. This is why we all need vision for our life. We need to see beyond the present to the future. If we want a future that does not look like our past, then we must consistently make new choices in the present.

Dr. Williams

Take a Journey

Create more vision in your life. Put up an old photo of yourself when you were more fit to remind yourself of what you are working for. Consider buying a pair of pants that is two sizes too small. Post a sign on your fridge that says, "Nothing tastes as good as skinny feels." Let this serve to remind you of the difference between short term and long-term pleasure.

ATTITUDE OF GRATITUDE

By Nicole Wilber

*"Don't mistake a bump in your Journey
for the end of the road."*

– Unknown

"It had been about 3 hours since we finished my mammogram. I'd seen dozens of women come and go. I hadn't been called yet. I stopped a nurse and asked if she would check my file. She promptly came back and told me I had to stay. The doctor wanted to see me. That can only mean one thing: Cancer. Devastation consumed me."

Looking back, Theresa thought she had already endured it all. After 27 years of marriage, her life was turned upside down when her husband passed away. She was 61 and now completely on her own. Theresa was suffering from diabetes, neuropathy, venous insufficiency, and constricted lung disease, resulting in the need for oxygen at night. One might think she was dealt an unlucky hand.

Feelings of isolation and loneliness left Theresa feeling trapped for many years until someone suggested Journey Fitness. A well-trained and knowledgeable staff makes Theresa feel like a priority. The emphasis on overall good health versus weight loss is important to her. She knew from the beginning that the benefits of this program would far outweigh the financial burden it would place on her. A shift in priorities was necessary.

What Theresa was not prepared for when she first began at Journey Fitness was the new family support she would gain. On her first day at Journey, Nancy Simons told her, "You need to get some workout clothes." This was the start of a lasting friendship. Nancy continued to push Theresa through every workout and continued to encourage her, regardless of her age and limitations.

Things were really looking up for Theresa. Her Journey was off to an amazing start. She was no longer on oxygen or needing breathing treatments. She lost over 20 pounds. She made significant improvements in her physical strength and mobility, and more importantly, her mental strength.

Then the day came when her Journey took a turn for the worse. She had just learned of her breast cancer diagnosis. She was silent the entire way home; not a word was exchanged between her and her sister-in-law. Theresa was in shock. She had no idea how this would change her life, but she knew it would never be the same. It was 2 weeks before she even told her family.

After learning of her new diagnosis, Theresa was more thankful than ever for her Journey Fitness family and supporters. She firmly believes that Journey played a major role in helping her through the recovery process, not just from a supportive standpoint, but the physical improvements she made helped tremendously.

Today, Theresa is preparing to have a knee replacement. For her, this is another bump in the road. Instead of focusing on the impact of another setback, she is thanking Journey Fitness for being alongside her every step of the way. She knows her recovery process from this new bump in the road will, again, be much faster thanks to Journey. She is now a devoted advocate for Journey Fitness and wants to share her experience as a cancer survivor to anyone it could help.

TAKE A JOURNEY

Gratitude is one of the most important qualities one can possess. It cannot be practiced enough. Strength is another. When you have an attitude of gratitude, you have strength. When you have trained your mind to focus on the positives, you can endure anything. Even when your Journey takes a turn for the worse and life is doing everything in its will to bring you to your knees, you don't waiver one bit. When you hold such a strong appreciation for your life and the people in it, it gives you a certain inner strength. What may seem like a giant battle to some, is just a bump in the road to others. It's not the end your Journey.

WHEN YOUR JOURNEY TAKES A TURN

By Wendy Lupo

*"I am ALL IN for life! I know I will stumble,
I know I will fall, and I know there will be my
Journey Fitness family to lift me up again."*

– Mary Beth Fiore

Mary Beth could see it but could not reach it. There it was, high up on the shelf in the garage, her box of golfing equipment. Excited to hit the course, she dragged out the ladder, turning it upright, pressing the hinges to secure it in place. Mary Beth had her eye on that box. Focused, she placed each foot securely, slowly moving up the rungs of the ladder. As she pulled the box from its place it caught, pushing her back, causing her to fall from the ladder to the hard concrete. The vibrancy, strength, and confidence gained, lost in one fall, literally crushed. Mary Beth would endure two shoulder surgeries and much rehabilitation, along with an eighteen-month hiatus from Journey Fitness. How would she ever get back what she had accomplished?

Growing up, Mary Beth was always active. She was a four-sport athlete at Auburn High School and played sports at Ithaca College. Then life happened - a trifecta as she described it! Mary Beth learned that she could not bear children, her relationship of thirteen years sadly ended, and during this time, she lost her parents at the ages of 60 and 65. She then immersed herself in her work. On the exterior she was in control, strong, confident and could successfully handle the challenges of her complex job responsibilities. Inside she felt inadequate, was self-doubting and insecure. Over the years, she had insulated herself with many layers and many extra pounds. Eight years ago, after a doctor's visit revealed she had high blood pressure, symptoms of a pre-diabetic, and sleep apnea, all of which could potentially be rectified with weight loss, Mary Beth got serious. She was turning forty-five. She couldn't imagine only living fifteen more years, to the age of 60 as her mother had.

Mary Beth had always been the care-giver in her family, never taking time for herself, never making herself a priority. It was time to make a change. She worked with her medical doctors and a nutritionist. She adopted a new life style to get her health back on track. Mary Beth lost eighty pounds only to struggle with shedding the last thirty. She became frustrated. It was then that Mary Beth found Journey Fitness. People around her were making phenomenal transformations. Perhaps she could too. And she did!

Mary Beth developed good habits in nutrition through journaling, and she became educated and accountable. More important were the connections, the common threads, and unique challenges of each of the members that helped her draw strength to be successful. This holistic approach that Journey Fitness follows had helped her to overcome her challenges. You see, in the end, Mary Beth earned her place on the Journey Wall of Fame with her very own poster which illustrated her inspiring transformation. She reached her goal and would now maintain. That was until that horrific fall.

Journey Fitness became part of her fiber and there was a significant sense of loss when she could not proceed with what had become as natural as taking a shower each morning. With calls, emails, and cards of encouragement while she was away, Mary Beth was ready to battle back. She remembers her first session of her return, being challenged physically with things that she could do easily prior to her fall. The greatest comeback, though, was nothing physical. With the help and encouragement from her trainers, she has learned to accept and embrace the restrictions, and to work through them. As she says, she is once again ALL IN! In one word, she is "EMPOWERED".

Take a Journey

The only goal you need to have is to be better tomorrow than you are today. What are you going to do to make that happen?

Small Steps Build Momentum

By Jeff Case

*"You can't get where you want to be on the couch,
easy is always there waiting for you."*

— JC

"Some people say they can't afford a membership at Journey Fitness. That may be the case for some, but I think that's more of an excuse. I believe that most people will pay for what they want. Hell, a lot of us spend more than a monthly membership on unhealthy snacks and meals a month. I'm actually saving money now since I have stopped eating out!" – Dave Douglas

Before Dave started at Journey Fitness, he was always tired and not happy about his overall health. The hardest part was making himself start. He thought about it over the weekend after the Journey Fitness coach JC encouraged us at his presentation to our company, The Hilliard Corporation. Dave really didn't decide until Monday morning because he was so nervous about going and working out. It had been over 20 years since his last work out and now he was going to do it in front of a bunch of co-workers, some that he knew were going to Journey Fitness for a while and were in good shape. Dave said, "And now here comes fat, out of shape Dave!"

Dave's nervousness quickly disappeared during his first workout as his focus became trying to just catch his breath and breathe better. This is how he started his Journey, with a weight loss challenge with some friends that were just as out of shape as he was.

It's very easy to get caught up in life's routine. That's where he was when I came to present the fitness challenge with the folks in Dave's plant. Dave runs the Cartridge plant in the Hilliard Corporation. One of the things that I mentioned to them was the opportunity to get off prescription medications which are the fourth leading cause of death in America. Dave's cholesterol and blood pressure were high. Dave felt that Hilliard and Journey Fitness made it too easy to not try it out and states that "JC makes you want to come back."

Dave is very proud of his two beautiful, athletic daughters, and he is close with them. He does a lot of activities with them, especially outdoors. Some of them were getting really difficult for him because he was physically out of shape. Besides that, Dave wants to be around for them for a few more decades. Who here would like to be around longer for their children?

When Dave started his Journey, he set a goal to lose 20 pounds. He thought that he would be happy with that even though he wasn't sure he could reach his goal. However, Dave did acknowledge that he couldn't get there by sitting in an office chair or on the couch. Once he started seeing results, it became easier for him to watch his diet and get to his workouts 5 days a week. Dave found that getting into an eating routine was a huge help for him. He also believes that we should hold ourselves accountable as well, and not necessarily on the coach or someone else. Dave states, "If I'm not seeing the results I want, it's my own fault."

It's been about 5 months since Dave started with Journey Fitness and he has lost over 30lbs. He is looking to set a new goal to work towards. I asked Dave what is going to help him reach his new goal and stick with it? To which he said, "JC's constant encouragement and seeing results from my hard work. I'm getting a little better every day and excited for all the new adventures to come with my beautiful daughters."

TAKE A JOURNEY

Dave believes that a workout is just like work, we just get paid in a different way. This is so true. People thrive from consistency and routine. If we look at our fitness and health goals like our job, where we have a schedule- get up and go whether we like to or not, routinely eat good whole foods, we will then make healthier habits that are easier to manage. It's when we feel out of routine that our health declines. Do something now that will get you one step closer to where you want to be. Small steps build momentum. Do it now!

ONE FOOT IN FRONT OF THE OTHER

By Nicole Wilber

"There are two ways to live your life. One is as though nothing is a miracle. The other is as though everything is a miracle."

– Albert Einstein

"It's been a few days since the accident and they told me I am now stable enough to transport. I will be going to Portland (Maine) for my second operation so they can put me back together, literally." It's been over 20 years since Janet's motorcycle accident, but every year, as the July 7th anniversary approaches, it is a tough time for her to recall.

181

Janet was an athlete her entire life. In college, she majored in elementary and physical education, with a concentration in exercise physiology. Later, she decided to take a slightly different route and work as a perfusionist. Working in the medical field, Janet had a daily reminder of the importance of taking care of herself. This is why she always made it a point to remain active. She even loved distance running.

In the blink of an eye, Janet's entire life changed, and it would never be the same again. Janet and her fiancé were on their motorcycle when they were hit head-on by a drunk driver. Her fiancé was killed instantly while Janet sustained very serious injuries, that often times, most people cannot survive. Janet, who used to run at least seven miles every day, would now spend the next month of her life in the hospital. The night of the accident she was placed on an external fixator. Her pubic bone was split four inches wide, later requiring a metal plate to hold it in place. She sustained injuries to her sacrum, hips, and nerves in her right leg, and more. Doctors told her she could not carry a child, nor would she ever run or jump again. She was out of work for two years and had a total of five surgeries related to the accident, including a hip replacement 20 years later. She lost 92 pounds due to stress and had to learn to walk all over again.

Janet tried for several years to get back into the gym to help gain her strength and confidence back. Nothing seemed to be working and she often felt discouraged.

Enter Journey Fitness. Janet has found a new motivation, and more importantly, a new family of support. She looks forward to new workouts each week and the encouragement from the coaches. It has been difficult for Janet, emotionally and physically, as she was so active before, and now describes herself as "handicapped" when she started Journey Fitness. She finds comfort in the fact that she is able to work to the best of her ability and not compete with other members in the class. She loves that other members, complete strangers, are routing for her as well. Every day she is getting stronger. It has been an incredibly long Journey toward recovery. Janet still has a long ways to go, but for someone who thought she would never walk again, she has made incredible strides! Janet often reminds herself of a quote from Calvin Coolidge, "Persistence and determination alone are omnipotent."

TAKE A JOURNEY

Cherish life, every day, and never give up. When someone tells you that you can't do something, show them you can. Keep a tenacious attitude and each day will be one foot in front of the other, even if they are baby steps.

IT'S NEVER TOO LATE

By Travis Barnes and Jeff Katz

"We are the makers of our own destiny,
and living a healthy lifestyle is the very best thing
I have done for me."

– Jeff Katz

Jeff Katz

I still remember being 17 years old lying in bed at 10:30PM on Tuesday night. We lived in a small apartment, which meant the rooms were all relatively close. I heard a loud thump in the bathroom. It was my father. He had a massive heart attack, and he was dead at the age 51, before he even hit the floor.

Now here I am at the age of 61, the heaviest I have ever been, regular cortisone shots in my knees to help with knee pain and re-occurring back problems just from bending down and tying my shoes. Heart disease more than likely runs in our family and I am not doing much to avoid it. I've tried different gyms - but saw no improvement.

In August 2013 I was physically and mentally at my lowest point. I noticed this Open House for Journey Fitness. Knowing nothing about it, I decided to drop in and had a chance to meet Travis. He explained to me about the program, and I decided, on the spot, to at least give it a try.

My initial assessment was with Cyndy. After my evaluation, Cyndy explained how the program worked and what Journey's commitment to me would be. She continued on to explain some things I did not expect which was what was expected of me - submit a food journal (weekly) and come to Journey three times a week. Having been through other programs, I was never asked to make a commitment. I knew right then that Journey Fitness was different, and I embraced as part of something. I very quickly learned I was part of something very special.

Beyond the exercise regime was an understanding about what to eat and how to incorporate a high protein low carb diet. As I saw the results, it all began to make a lot of sense. I began eating smaller portions and breaking up the day with smaller meals and snacks and removed virtually all starches and desserts. I did not even touch alcohol until I hit my goal.

It took me about 18 months to reach my goal of losing fifty pounds, but the more rewarding goal has been to keep it off as I move towards my 4th year at Journey. It is, indeed, a Journey, and I am so thrilled I decided to be part of Journey Fitness.

Clearly the one thing I do believe is it is never too late to change your lifestyle. The quality of my life has changed dramatically. Having just turned 65, I can't remember a time in the past 25 years where I have felt as physically and mentally fit as I am today. We are the makers of our own destiny, and living a healthy lifestyle is the very best thing I have done for "me".

Jeff Katz and Todd Durkin

TAKE A JOURNEY

It's never too late to become what you might have been. Would the boy or girl you once were, be proud of the man or woman you are today? If not, how can you commit more fully to the change you need to make to become the person you want to become?

TAKE A DIFFERENT PATH

By Nicole Wilber

"A bend in the road is not the end of the road...
unless you fail to make the turn."

– Helen Keller

Three hundred and eight pounds. Fat and out of shape. Depressed and frustrated. This was Chris, before Journey Fitness. Chris had been given many opportunities to just give up- a partial knee replacement, a repaired ankle, degenerative arthritis in his hip, significant lumbar degenerative arthritis due to sciatica, and numerous stents to keep his heart beating. To top things off, a ventricular tachycardia was his latest diagnosis. Simply put, episodes of irregular heartbeat.

Chris, a firefighter, experienced his first episode while on the job. Unsure of what was happening, he brushed it off as just an anxiety attack. Still not feeling up to par, Chris participated in a fishing tournament the next day. The feeling was worse. The only way he could describe it was, "It's like someone struck you with a baseball bat in the chest, with all his or her might." Chris went straight to the hospital after the tournament, where he first heard of his new condition. Chris knew he had a long road ahead of him. He was forced to retire from firefighting. After tragedy struck our small town, which directly affected Chris and family, he was at an all-time low. His good friend, Rich Weed, had been trying for some time to get him to come to Journey Fitness. Chris would laugh and say, "I don't need that cornball shit."

Though he would laugh at Richie's suggestion, deep down, Chris understood the severity of his heart condition. He had already endured one major open-heart surgery, requiring him to be awake the entire time. Though his surgery was successful, it was the third hospital that had attempted. The first hospital backed out after two hours under the knife. The second backed out after six hours. The third hospital successfully completed Chris' surgery after 16.5 hours. His doctor said he would need to lose 100 pounds before his next surgery. Not knowing where else to turn, he came to Journey with Rich and made a 12-month commitment on the spot.

Chris' health has done a complete 180 since starting Journey Fitness. Instead of waking up, already exhausted, he is now waking up energized and going to bed exhausted from a full day. Chris says the changes he has experienced are unbelievable. Today he is down about 50 pounds and striving to lose another 50. His wife has lost 20 pounds simply because she follows Chris' nutrition plan. She has realized the importance of this Journey for Chris' health and does all she can to stick with him and support him. Chris has gone from a sedentary lifestyle, to looking forward to his workouts. So much so, that there are days he works out twice a day. Chris immediately fit right into the Journey Fitness family. He thrives on the camaraderie and truly feels he is supported beyond just his weight loss Journey.

Take a Journey

We are all trying to get through this thing called life, day by day. It's a rollercoaster, as they say, full of ups and downs. One day out of nowhere, life swings that baseball bat with such force your entire world is turned upside down. Sometimes, though, that's all we need; to look at life from a different perspective. Looking from a different angle changes the direction our Journey is heading. When that baseball bat hits you and it feels like the end of the Journey, a new path is exactly what you need.

Commitment

By Wendy Lupo

*"We all must travel the distance
of a lifetime in this body. If we do not care for it,
how can we reach our goals?"*

– Swami Kripalu

Bob and Phil Mrkus before

Why get excited about retirement if we won't be able to enjoy it? It seems we spend all our lives working hard, providing for, protecting, and supporting our family, saving and looking forward to the retirement years. All the while, we forget to take care of ourselves. We are rarely a priority.

193

Bob and Philomena (better known to most as Phil), married thirty-seven years and now both retired, entered the doors of Journey Fitness in 2015. Their goals? "We wanted to be able to enjoy retirement together, have happy adventures, actively spend time with our daughter and son-in-law, be prepared for (cross our fingers) grandchildren to come, and ultimately be healthier." Over the years, they had forgotten themselves and were ready to commit to a healthy retirement.

Bob and Phil made that commitment to Journey Fitness despite the time it would take, the sweat it would create, and the money it would cost. "It is like a full-time job," says Phil. "One that pays well, though."

Phil describes Journey as an "old soul". Like an old soul, Journey Fitness recognizes that we have a beautiful lifetime ahead of us on this planet. The old soul, like Journey, has a plan and a purpose for us being here. "Everything came together for us at Journey-functional fitness, the readings after workouts, the camaraderie of members and the support of the trainers," explains Phil.

Since joining the Journey family, together Bob and Phil have lost a total of 135 pounds. Bob, in his early years, was an avid down-hill skier and runner. He enjoys challenges and is competitive, but his concentration is on himself not others. He has gotten back into running as he wanted, and even took a Chi running class, given by a Journey member, that improved his form. He has decreased his time per mile and has had no injuries with running now, unlike when he was younger. Phil is more of a short-term goal, baby step, kind of a lady. She was just looking to survive the workouts and, at first, enjoyed doing just the regressions. Now of course, you may see her doing the super band assisted pull-ups.

"Who would have thought?" she says. While Phil is happy hitting the two-minute plank and walking 5ks, Bob is running half and full marathons, sometimes with snow hanging from his eyebrows.

They may have different fitness goals but one thing is very evident and that is the support they share for one another. Phil supports Bob in his longer races, cheering him on no matter the elements and is the head of the nutrition at home. Bob says it is more important to spend time together so he doesn't always run the shorter races. He will walk them so they can be together. They also have been known to take part in the fitness challenges together. One time, for Halloween, Phil dressed as a pilgrim and Bob as the turkey. They enjoy lots of fun and laughs! That is the ultimate-goal… to enjoy time together. Time they both deserve.

Bob and Phil Mrkus after

TAKE A JOURNEY

"We don't stop playing because we grow old; we grow old because we stop playing."

– George Bernard Shaw

Commitment is determining that no excuse is good enough. It is making what you want most more important than what you want now.

PERSEVERE

By Nicole Wilber

"Faith allows things to happen. It is the power that comes from a fearless heart. And when that fearless heart believes...miracles can happen."

– Christianne, brain tumor survivor

Debby Thomson

"Arterio vascular malformation, a birth defect, had taken control of my life. Since 2006, I had been in and out of brain surgery. My first open brain surgery was scheduled for September of 2015. This would complete my healing process."

Between the cocktail of medications and the on again, off again exercise regime, Debby found herself 80 pounds heavier before her open brain surgery. She kept her focus solely on getting through each surgery. She counted her blessings every day and was hopeful her life would return to some normalcy after weeks of recovery. Going into the final steps before surgery was like preparing for battle, as Debby recalls. She wanted to be more physically fit to speed up her recovery. Her dear friend, Chris Baxter, had been coming to Journey Fitness for quite a while and had seen amazing results. Debby decided to join. In her first 2 months, she was down 20 pounds and feeling great. She felt stronger, motivated and had plenty of faith-filled supporters. A few of the ladies even went to her house for breakfast, really lifting Debby's spirits. She was hopeful she would return to Journey Fitness post surgery, as she needed the camaraderie, kindness and caring attitude of the Journey staff and her new found family.

Six months after surgery Debby returned to Journey, mentally and physically drained. The surgery left the right side of her body very weak. Therapy was required for an extensive time. Travis and Cyndy, the owners of Journey Fitness, worked alongside Debby and her physical therapist in order to modify workouts so Debby could return on her Journey. This meant the world to Debby, that the owners were dedicated to helping her continue her healing Journey.

Debby's first day back at Journey was the first of many days that brought tears. Nicole, a coach who she had become very close with, was there through the tears. She told Debby she was a very courageous and strong woman. She encouraged her to do what her body would allow. That's all that mattered. Instead of perfection is what Debby needed in that moment. Over the next 6 months she lost 14 pounds. Though it was slow, Debby was making great strides physically and mentally.

In February of 2017 Debby returned to work at Corning Community College. Journey continues to be a mainstay in her life. She has grown closer with several coaches who are deeply routed in their Christian faith. These relationships have served as a huge stepping-stone toward healing. Today, Debby's blood pressure is back to normal. Every day she is gaining strength, mentally and physically. She has significantly cut back on her anti-depressant medication, originally prescribed when her five senses were compromised due to surgery. She says, "Journey Fitness is more than just squats, pride claps and hurricanes. It encourages unity! We do life together! We are vulnerable together! We have a relationship. That's what motivates me." Debby is committed to her goals and thankful for her Journey every day. She says, "I commit to new goals every 3 months or so, whether it's increasing my workouts, getting on the floor more, using heavier weights, moving my legs faster, or just challenging myself to do better. I am doing it...even if it's one step at a time."

TAKE A JOURNEY

It always seems that people with the greatest hardships come out the strongest. What's important is to remain positive, no matter the hand you're dealt. As they say, an arrow can only be shot by first pulling it backwards. Remember that, the next time you are experiencing a "set back."

JUST DECIDE

By Jeff Case

"Make a choice. Like, you just decide.
What's it going to be, who you're going to be,
how you're going to do it. Just decide."

– Will Smith

Have you ever woken up one morning to get dressed and go to work only to realize that you went up a notch in your belt buckle? Have you ever given up a bad habit only to gain weight? Have you ever thought it was too late in life to lose 40 pounds?

Meet Gene and Debby.

It was early 2016. Debby was sound asleep but Gene had woken up a little earlier than normal. He decided to get up to use the bathroom. As he turned the corner, he noticed the cold metallic grey weight scale sitting underneath the vanity. It appeared to be dusty. Gene thought to himself, "It really has been a while since

I've checked my weight." So, he reluctantly inched his way over to the scale and bent over. He dusted off the digital screen and then stepped on. The scale was cold under his feet. The numbers were rising. Gene thought to himself, this can't be right. I'm 30 pounds heavier than I was six years ago.

Gene noticed his wardrobe had become quite tight and realized that either he had to buy new clothes or do something about it. And he didn't mean in a good way.

Sometimes we lose sight of how out of shape we can become, and how quickly! Both Gene and his wife Debby had given up smoking and gained weight, but never realized how much had really accumulated! They did the Weight Watchers thing for four years and lost the weight, but not the bad habits. As a result, the weight crept back. When Debby came in to Journey for her intake, her knees were in very bad shape, and her stamina was meager. Gene was in better physical shape, but his snack attacks were his undoing. Gene was always an athlete, but with bad eating habits.

In the 15 months since Gene and Debby first signed up for Journey Fitness, they both experienced a total change, not just in their physical selves, but their daily lives as well. They have two furry friends and three grandchildren who keep them young. Whether it's the long walks on the dike with their animals or keeping up with their grandkids, their (P.R.I.D.E.): personal responsibility in their daily efforts, has given them energy they need and it has paid off big time. A year ago, they were walking their dogs separately. Now they get up to walk them together morning and night. They join each other for their noon time workouts five times a week. Gene is now eating spaghetti squash! A year ago Debby would have laughed at the thought! Gene is down 45 pounds, Debby 30 and that is 75 pounds total!

Being a team has improved every facet of Gene and Debby's lives and they love how they've become better together every step of the way!

Here is what Gene and Debby had to say about Journey Fitness:

"We believe that the individual attention, the modifications to compensate for ability, and the teamwork really help to make this program a success. The nutrition tips, the encouragement, and the connection that is made between trainers and clients all come together to make a perfect storm. We have found that 'you' set your limits, and that positive input brings positive output! We are at a point in our lives where we want to enjoy retirement, not watch life go by, and Journey Fitness has helped us to enjoy each day to the fullest."

Gene and Debby Before

TAKE A JOURNEY

Just decide. Decide that at the end of the day your life matters. Your spouse's life matters. Be a Rockstar like Gene and Debby. Take action, move forward to create the best version of yourself for you, your family, and relationships. We are better together!

MIRACLES HAPPEN

By Nicole Wilber

*"Just when I think I have learned
the way to live, life changes."*

– Hugh Prather

"It was like someone had hit me in the head with a bat. I made my way to the bathroom to get some aspirin. I realized I was having trouble walking. I collapsed on my bed where I remained, helpless. The entire right side of my body was paralyzed. The CAT scan revealed a partly ruptured aneurysm. Once they told me they could not operate, due to it's location on my brain, my mind went a mile a minute, in every direction imaginable. Little did I know, this would be the best thing to ever happen to me."

As Carol spent several weeks in the hospital recovering, she had a lot of time to think. She started thinking about all the things she had yet to do with her life. One of the most important things was taking her daughters to Disney, as she had always promised they would someday go. Though she was now on a tight budget and very limited with her physical abilities, Carol wasted no time going to the travel agent following her release from the hospital. She booked the trip to Disney. The travel agents, knowing a bit about Carol's situation, pulled a few strings. This trip was certainly one to remember. When Carol and family got to their room, it was stocked with snacks and beverages, and decked out with stuffed animals and autographed Disney gear. The park manager gave the family passes to cover the duration of their stay. The travel agents had even arranged for Carol to receive an electric wheel chair since her mobility was severely limited now.

Every day Carol strives to get stronger. She believes she still has a long way to go, but has made some amazing progress. She is thankful she discovered Journey Fitness, as it has completely changed her mindset. She looks forward to her workouts and nutrition sessions where she has already learned so much. Her balance and strength are improving every day. She is thankful for the coaches that encourage her and always offer helpful, genuine advice. Carol is thankful for her new mindset, as she knows not to take a single day for granted. Every day is a gift.

Take a Journey

At one time or another, we all think we are invincible. We think we are pardoned from certain things, certain situations. "That could never happen to me," we tell ourselves. Truth be told, tomorrow is not promised. Live in the moment. Don't wait. Been thinking about making a change in your life? Do it. Been thinking about offering a compliment to someone? Say it. Been thinking about taking a vacation? Book it. Don't wait. The moment is not perfect; it's never going to be. Cherish every minute you have on this earth.

PERFORM BETTER

THERE IS NO SUCH WORD AS CAN'T

By Travis Barnes

*"Don't ever let someone tell you
that you can't do something."*

— **Will Smith** - from the movie Pursuit of Happiness

Not many people actually know what they want to be when they grow up. The majority of us simply avoid the things we don't want to do and follow the path before us. Fred was different. He knew his path from age 6. It was then that he would stand waiting for the school bus, looking at books on the history of artillery. All Fred ever wanted to be was a paratrooper and Green Beret. Most importantly Fred never stopped to wonder if it was possible.

Fred entered the Special Forces Army Selection with 180 fellow soldiers. After months of rigorous testing, 22 soldiers were selected and Fred was one of them. Fred says, "*My first and foremost greatest moment is when I earned the right to bear the Green Beret*". Each Green Beret must choose between 4 divisions: Weapons, Engineering & Demolitions, Communications or Medical.

Fred chose to become a Special Forces Medic and he served our country for over 12 years before meeting his wife Erin. It was challenging having a wife while going on secret missions for the military. One time Fred returned home very sick with Malaria. Erin asked Fred why he was doing what he was doing. He looked around and realized he was old the guy. He then realized that he might have bought a one-way ticket. Remembering the college option he got when he signed on, Fred decided to go back to college to become a doctor while serving in the ROTC.

Again Fred did not stop to consider if he could really do it because in Fred's language there is no such word as *Can't*. Fred completed his 4-year undergrad degree in 2 years by taking more credits than were allowable. He did this by signing up as 2 different students. Fredrick Teribury Jr went to school during the day and

Fred Teribury went to school at night. His days were long from 5:30am til 11:30pm. After 4 more years of medical school and 18 years of military service, Fred left the military to become a civilian doctor.

Fred is currently the lead physician for the Corning Guthrie hospital and he has never stopped serving our country. Fred continues to support our troops through a private company that travels to the Middle East to provide medical support.

Not long ago Fred found out he had an aneurysm in his aorta which meant immediate surgery and complete rest. Fred describes his surgery by saying "they split my chest open, took my heart out, cut off my aorta and replaced with Dacron tube which is type of artificial aorta." It was several months before Fred could return to light duty. The doctor who did Fred's surgery said he should be able to do everything he did before which was great for Fred who did not understand the word *Can't*.

When it was nearing time for Fred to return to work, he came to Journey Fitness to work on his cardiovascular fitness. He had been to Journey Fitness before. In fact, he had trained with Travis and Cyndy before there was a Journey Fitness. Fred liked the way the workouts reminded him of the workouts he did as a Green Beret. He also liked that fact that now Journey Fitness offered a heart rate monitoring device called MyZone.

Fred approached his workouts with the same effort and determination as he did everything else. He never stopped to think, "I *Can't* do this." Fred not only returned to work but he was also cleared to return to his work in the Middle East. Fred remembers his first trip stating, "*I was up for my first mission to Afghanistan. Upon arrival to the terminal in Kabul I was identified by one of the personnel and informed that I was to proceed immediately outside as one of my medics was awaiting me. When I walked out and saw my old friend "Dino" he verbally confirmed that I was physically fit and ready to run.*

The incoming terminal is on one end of the runway and the operational area is on the other. He handed me body armor. He then kindly grabbed my carry-on and said let's go. We just got scrambled for a medi-vac mission and a chopper is warming up on the ramp. If you've ever looked at the length of an international runway then you can likely imagine the run that took place. Old friendships and camaraderie aside, I was tested for my own benefit as well as the safety of my team members. There cannot be a weak link in the chain. At the finish line I was greeted with a hot blast from the helicopter's jet turbines. Running up the halo's ramp, I was welcomed home to that place I was called to be since I was 6 years old. The Medevac pick up and transport to Bagram air base hospital was successful."

Take a Journey

Are we destined to do some things or if we believe, can we do anything? I guess no really knows the answer to that. All we know is we should follow that passion and don't ever let anyone tell you that you Can't do something. One more thought from Fred, *"In the deepest darkest times of my Journey my thoughts have always been that I will laugh and enjoy again." I hope you believe that too, and hope you never use the word "can't."*

I WILL

By Jeff Case

"I may not be there yet,
but I'm closer than I was yesterday."

– Lindsay Kolk

It was coming up on Mother's Day 2016. Lindsay, the mother of three beautiful children, felt uncomfortable in her own skin. She had gained a lot of weight over the past few years due to a combination of life events, including being diagnosed with Celiac's disease, her marriage ending, and going back to college. On top of that, in April of 2016, her ex-husband and father of her children had a stroke. Lindsay saw what could happen if she continued to live the way she was living, so she decided to do something different. She took the opportunity to join Journey Fitness. She knew it was going to be hard, but she also knew it was going to be worth it.

As part of our fitness consultation at Journey Fitness we ask our clients what three things they will do to succeed as part of their accountability process. We call these our "I Will" statements.

Lindsay made a commitment to herself and her coaches that she would go to Journey Fitness three times a week, make healthy food choices, and journal everything she ate. Her first workout was hard and she had to take many breaks. Lindsay remembers that she could only do one squat thrust during a 35 second round. She also remembers not being able to do a full pushup and only holding a plank for 45 seconds during our performance testing at Journey Fitness. She was very sore, but credited the amazing coaches and members who worked out regularly for encouraging her to come back. It was that reassurance from people who were sharing the same interest and goal that Lindsay needed to help her get better.

But then something happened to Lindsay. It started to get a little easier for her. Over the course of 2 weeks, Lindsay found that she needed less breaks and could keep up. She started to realize that, on the days that she woke up at 4am to be a part of the 5am class, she had more energy and her attitude was better. It was then that Lindsay decided that if her days at Journey Fitness first thing in the morning were so much better, then it didn't make sense for her to not go every morning.

Over the next months, Lindsay didn't miss a day. She pushed herself as hard as she could. She told herself that if she was going to get her butt up this early each day, that she was going to make it worth it by giving it her all. Lindsay constantly pushed herself by grabbing weights that were one level heavier then she thought she could handle.

In September 2016 Lindsay ran her first 5k in Elmira Heights called the Hero Run. Lindsay couldn't run the whole time, but the friends at Journey Fitness encouraged her and cheered her on with "Hoorahs" and "Oh yeas" to a 45-minute finish. She was determined to get better so she signed up for her next 5k in November. It was the Turkey Trot at the Elmira Notre Dame High School, and she completed it in 39 minutes. That was six minutes faster than her first! Wow, very impressive. Lindsay has never been a runner, but every day she puts one foot in front of the other and persistently keeps striving for more.

So much more that Lindsay became obsessed with becoming a Journey Fitness Spartan. She had her eye on the first ever winter spartan in the U.S. It was here at Greek Peak ski resort in our local town of Cortland, N.Y. Lindsay got it in her head that she wanted to be a part of that Journey Fitness Spartan Team. She trained as hard as she could. She ran when running was the last thing she wanted to do. She did two-a-days at Journey Fitness whenever she could. Lindsay was scared, but determined.

At the finish line, there was our Journey Fitness Team waiting for everyone to jump over the last obstacle to complete this frozen tundra. Her legs were on fire and finally it hit her. Lindsay was feeling incredible, exhausted but relieved and accomplished She did it!

Lindsay said, "I will never forget what it felt like crossing the finish-line. I was hooked."

Something Lindsay has heard before that she applies to her Journey is, "If the goal doesn't scare you, then you didn't set it high enough."-unknown

Since that race, Lindsay has continued to work hard and push herself each day. So far, Lindsay has lost nearly 100 pounds, but for the first time in her life Lindsay says, "it's not about the number on the scale or a pants size, it's about reaching for better. I can run a 5k in under 30 minutes now, I've completed a Spartan Beast of 12 plus miles in more mud than I knew even existed and will be racing in at least 2 more Spartans this year; completing my Spartan Trifecta. During Hurricane Week, I can now do 33 perfect push-ups and hold a 2-minute plank. But the most important thing is how I feel. I feel better in my mid-30's than I ever did in my 20's. My blood sugar is extremely stable, my Celiac's is in check, I have the energy to chase after and play with my kids, and I feel so much stronger and confident than I have ever been before!"

Lindsay Kolk Before and After with JC

TAKE A JOURNEY

Something we can all take away from Lindsay's story is her unwavering grit. Let's not forget that Lindsay was scared and nervous all the time. However her will to win and her commitment to herself has pushed her far beyond her limits and expectations. Lindsay is an inspiration and example of the Tim Duncan quote, "Good, Better, Best. Never let it rest. Until your good gets better and your better gets best!"

RESILIENCE

By Logan Peters

*"I am not what happened to me,
I am what I choose to become."*

– Carl Gustav Jung

Laying in a hospital bed, Danny couldn't feel the left side of his face, and he could barely eat on his own. He had just had his second TIA (Mini Stroke). His first TIA had happened three years prior leaving him unable to walk or run as he enjoyed. Fortunately, after weeks of physical therapy his ability to walk returned. Yet, running was still out of the question and now he had just suffered his second TIA. With the side effects of the second stroke, Danny also found he started to gain weight. Danny stated his weight jumped 20 pounds and he didn't understand why.

Prior to these two TIA's Danny was a relatively active person. He loved running which he started when he was in high school. Throughout his running career Danny experienced knee injuries here and there. Unlike most, he found running was the only thing that helped the knee pain subside. When he was in the military

223

he ran every day, he ran two marathons in Buffalo, NY and he would even run in all-weather conditions including winter races. This was a major part of his life.

Then it was taken away when he had his first stroke. Here was a man who ran for most of his life and now could no longer run. Danny could have easily made a choice to give up or lose hope of an active life again. But, with the help of his wife and regaining the ability to use his legs through PT, Danny was able to start some exercises at the Ithaca College Wellness Clinic. This was good, but Danny was finding it hard to lose the weight he had gained. Also, his balance continued to be an issue.

Then one day his daughter joined a challenge at Journey Fitness. Soon after, his wife also joined to lose weight. At this time, he was able to adopt his wife's new eating habits which started to impact his weight for the better. Danny then found himself trying out a class at Journey Fitness. At first it was very hard for him due to the effects of the two strokes. Just learning the coordination of the exercises was challenging because of the TIA. That didn't stop Danny, though. He started to find tricks which helped him learn the exercises, and he knew to do only what he could. With time Danny was able to learn to jump again, exercises became a little easier to perform and his balance had improved. Although some agility exercises still give him trouble, Danny continues to push forward.

For Danny, it was more than health and wellness. It was a battle for his life. Not giving up on his pursuit of an active life has allowed Danny to go from 204 pounds to 188. He's regained enjoyment in the activities he is now able to do. He gets to continue supporting his wife's health by being by her side at each workout, and hopes this will allow him to eliminate or reduce some of the medications he is currently taking as his Journey continues!

TAKE A JOURNEY

Life throws us many obstacles- some harder than others. We must be resilient in our actions by never giving up on ourselves and the ones around us. We have a choice to make the best of our situation and giving up is not an option.

THE JOURNEY IS BETTER TOGETHER

by Jesse King

"Encourage each other and build each other up."

— 1 Thessalonians 5:11.

Before joining Journey Fitness, Katy Prince was doing a lot of what she refers to as "deep chair sitting." Katy wasn't obese, but had been trying for quite a while to lose just 15 pounds. She had been trying on her own, and felt she was failing miserably. She was discouraged to the point where she was doing less exercise at home and more "deep chair sitting" in front of the TV. The day the Wii told her she was overweight, she wanted to throw it out the window.

It's natural to lose the motivation and desire to exercise, especially when you're not seeing any progress. It's natural to want to quit when you're lacking support and encouragement. This is where having a coach, a workout partner, or family member to help push you through the tough times can be so valuable. Fortunately for Katy she has a very supportive husband.

When Katy first asked her husband, Tommy, if he would go to Journey Fitness, he said yes because he wanted to support her. Tommy noticed that she was trying to lose weight on her own and not being successful. She was frustrated and he wanted to help.

Since joining Journey Fitness both Tommy and Katy have reached their long-term goals, and have pictures on the Wall of Fame in Ithaca. Tommy says, "The coaches have been an enormous influence and source of encouragement for me along with my family to be successful."

The Prince family exudes encouragement. They're a prime example of how a fitness family functions. A fitness family, similar to a church family, cares for each other, holds each other accountable, and makes fitness fun for each other. Most importantly they seek out opportunities to be a support and encouragement for others who might be struggling.

Shortly after joining, Tommy and Katy invited their daughter, Danielle, to a workout. Before coming to Journey Fitness Danielle tried to lose weight unsuccessfully many times. She felt miserable, and unmotivated. When Danielle came to her first workout she was determined to keep up with her mom - especially since Katy told Danielle that she was determined to look better than her daughters in a bathing suit when they went to the beach that summer. Danielle took that as challenge accepted and was determined to not let that happen. In fact, since joining Journey Fitness Danielle has reached her long-term goal, has her poster on the Wall of Fame next to her parents, and has a before and after picture in her bathing suit. Danielle says that it was her parents' initial influence on her attitude and eating habits that helped her to be successful.

Katy acknowledges that it's a lot of fun sharing this experience with her family. She says her biggest support in her transformation has been her husband, and running close behind him has been her children. The coaches have been an enormous influence and encouragement for her and her friend, Angie, who has been a great motivator for her as well. Watching Angie (and others in the class) has been very motivational and inspirational for Katy.

Exercise and eating healthy are two simple concepts, but practicing them both successfully on your own can be a very hard task to manage. It's for this very reason that we say at Journey Fitness that there's power in the group, and the Journey is better together.

TAKE A JOURNEY

1 Thessalonians 5:11, "Encourage each other and build each other up." And in the words of Katy, "Once someone has been an encouragement to you and influenced you, it is your turn to find someone else that needs that encouragement and motivation. Be determined to be the best you can be while doing so. You are stronger than you know and more cared for than you can imagine. You've got this!"

RELENTLESS

By Jeremy Purifoy

"Unity is strength... When there is teamwork and collaboration wonderful things can be achieved."

– Mattic Stpanek

Laura Carney - Before

I felt like my life was going a mile a minute. I hold a demanding job for one of the most prestigious companies in the world. While being in graduate school, and traveling 2 hours to work each day. I had to make a change! The first time that I walked through the doors at Journey Fitness I was scared! I do not like admitting that I have my weaknesses, and for me, my weight has always been a weakness. Although, I was confident in many aspects of my life, I was not confident about the way I looked. I did not like the way I felt about what I saw in the mirror. I felt like my appearance did not reflect the person inside. Not to mention, physically, I was exhausted all the time.

The person I am now, is pretty much the same person inside, but with a lot more confidence on the outside. I love meeting new people, making new friends and connecting with people at Journey. The confidence I now have on the outside has enabled me to be more successful at work, make friends in the community and conquer a lot of challenges I never dreamed of before, like pull-ups, Spartan Races, several 5Ks and a half marathon.

There were many motivations to change. I did not like the way I felt about what I saw, I wanted to look and feel beautiful, and at the time I did not feel this way. I had many stress factors in my life, I was starting my second year of my MBA, I was Project Manager at work for a large project, and was commuting from Rochester to Corning. Because of all these stressors in my life, I needed some way to cut it back! I needed to find a way to be more productive with the little time that I had, and I hoped along with the Journey that a by-product would be looking and feeling better.

At the beginning, I made sure I attended at least three sessions a week. After three weeks of consistency, I saw results. I then decided to take it a step further and follow the Low-Carb diet and use a food journal. That made a huge difference in my results. I was able to consistently lose weight week after week even though I was faced with many challenges like traveling,  and parties (through the holidays, those are always tough)! My personal accountability is what made me successful. I do not like excuses. I do not like it when people use excuses to blame not seeing results. For me, I know what I am doing right and what I am doing wrong, and I know I have the best results following a low-carb lifestyle and journaling every day in MyFitnessPal. Now that I am going into my third year as a Journey Fitness member, what I love the most is the members, and the sense of community. I feel great with the workouts, challenging myself and others, but with that being said I am motivated by my friends at Journey.

Do not worry about what everyone else is doing, focus on you and your results. When I am working out I focus on me, my form, and being better than I was yesterday, and that works! Today I live by being the silent motivator. I challenge myself while challenging my peers that are around me. I have lost over 50 plus pounds and yet my Journey is just beginning. Every day is another day to get better!

TAKE A JOURNEY

Accountability is the glue that ties commitment to results. If you want it bad enough you will hold yourself accountable to get there.

WHEN LIFE SHAKES YOU UP

By Jeff Case

"Stop waiting to get better
and start working to get Better!"

– Dan Ike

D an was diagnosed with chronic Lyme disease about 5 years ago after waking in the middle of the night in full AV block. His heart rhythm was going crazy and at first the doctors thought he may need a pace maker. He spent a week in the hospital and it really scared him and his family. There is no cure for Lyme Disease and treatment is pretty much a steady dose of anti-inflammatories, steroids and antibiotics. While the medications helped Dan they also took a toll on his body. Dan said, "It's easy to get down and frustrated when dealing with a chronic illness."

Dan finally reached the point where he was tired of waiting for his body to get better with medication and decided it was time to fight back. Dan decided to join Journey Fitness at his work in the Hilliard Corporation. After watching his co-workers get better through the program he was inspired to join. He started to think that maybe while he couldn't cure his Lyme Disease, he could beat it down a little if he was stronger and healthier... and then it happened again.

It was November 1st 2016 and Dan was about two months into the program with Journey Fitness. He spent part of the morning bow-hunting in the woods behind his house, and then went to work.

At work, Dan was feeling okay and made plans to work out with his co-worker at the noon class. Around 11:30am as Dan headed to his office he was stopped by a co-worker with a question. Suddenly, as he was standing there he felt a sensation like cold ice water running down the left side of his body. This was followed by a headache and instant numbness on his left side. At this point he tried to walk to a chair to sit down but couldn't move his left leg or arms. His co-worker realized something was wrong and asked if he needed medical help. Dan could only get out the words, "I think I'm having a stroke", before he collapsed to the floor.

Dan laid there conscious but unable to move. His first thought was panic that he had lost the use of his limbs and possibly worse. Luckily this all happened at work and not in the morning when he was alone in the woods. Medical attention was quick and he was to the hospital within minutes. The staff at the hospital immediately set about getting a brain scan and evaluating him for stroke. Less than 45 minutes from the time of the initial symptoms the doctors determined that Dan indeed did have a stroke and elected to treat him with the clot busting stroke drug, tPA. Results of the treatment were quick with feeling returning to his limbs and he was moved to ICU that evening. While recovering with his family by his side, Dan was surprised to see his coach and friend from Journey Fitness, JC, walk in to visit with him.

At this point he was moving his arm and leg again and began plotting his return to the gym. He felt that the two months of getting more fit at Journey Fitness helped play a huge role in his recovery. Dan left the hospital 3 days later with no visible signs of what he had just been through. Two weeks after his stroke, and doctor's release, he returned to work and his Journey Fitness workouts. Since then he has continued his workouts 4-5 times a week and continues to get stronger. When Dan first joined Journey Fitness he was overweight but more importantly he felt weak and old! Today Dan has lost over 50 lbs. He feels stronger and better than he has in years. Dan believes, "It is important to me to be there for my family and to be a strong Father/Husband that they can count on for years to come. Being healthy is the key and the support from Journey Fitness is helping me accomplish this."

Dan Ike and his trainer, JC

TAKE A JOURNEY

"When life shakes you up, you've gotta shake back."

– JC

Sometimes in life we get shaken up and sometimes we get slammed. It is these times that really define us. You realize you only have control of how you react to the trials and tribulations of life. Like Dan, we need to shake back and slam back at life. His auto-immune disease is terrifyingly imprecise. Tomorrow isn't promised. Darren Hardy articulates, "Your past has given you muscles, not wounds." The past struggles of life have made you stronger for today. Give your everything today because there might not be tomorrow.

YOUR GREATEST PAIN CAN BE YOUR GREATEST STRENGTH

By Travis Barnes

"Fitness is a Journey. Not a Destination"

– Kenneth H. Cooper

Shannon VanSkiver – Before   Shannon VanSkiver - After

In a recent article entitled, *"The Weight of Evidence,"* Harriet Brown reported *"your chance of keeping weight off for five years or more is about the same as your chance of surviving metastatic lung cancer: 5 percent.... In reality, 97 percent of dieters regain everything they lost and then some within three years. Obesity research fails to reflect this truth because it rarely follows people for more than 18 months."*

That is just the article of one person and their perspective on certain evidence, but it is worth paying attention. This article points out that weight maintenance is more difficult than weight loss. My hypothesis is that this difficulty exists because of the psychology of the motivation involved. Think about it. Weight loss usually begins because *"the pain of staying the same outweighs the pain of change."* – Henry Cloud. It happens when you can no longer stand your reflection in the mirror or your vital statistics give you a wake up call. That is when most are motivated to change but what about weight maintenance? What motivates us to stay the same when there is no longer a painful reflection staring back at you. In fact when you like what you see quite often the motivation is replaced by a belief that you deserve a treat.

Another negative with the psychology of maintenance is there isn't the same level of encouragement. When you are losing weight people say *"Hey! You're looking good! I can see the weight loss!"* But when you're maintaining no one says *"Hey! You're looking good! I can tell you are maintaining!"*

So there it is. Did you catch it? The secret to losing weight and keeping it off is staying in touch with the pain that got us to change in the first place, then continuing to encourage ourselves.

"Life is very interesting….in the end, some of your greatest pains become your greatest strengths." Drew Barrymore

Shannon VanSkiver is an example of how to say in touch with that pain to maintain her success. Twenty-four years ago Shannon weighed 261 pounds. She didn't like what she saw in the mirror. She was always worried about what others thought of her. She had been heavy most of her life. She still has hurtful memories of being called names such as "Mack Truck" because her maiden name was Mack. When she made a decision to change, she lost 115 pounds in 12 months and has kept that weight off for 23 years.

Shannon Vanskiver walked through the doors of Journey Fitness 4 years ago after maintaining her weight loss for 19 years. She says *"It wasn't that I had weight to lose, but more so I needed the help and a plan to become stronger, build muscle, gain speed and endurance with my running and most importantly ditch the demons so I could have more confidence in myself."*

It's no coincidence that Shannon walked through the doors of Journey Fitness after she started running 5ks. Subconsciously Shannon had been keeping the weight off with negative reinforcement keeping those negative memories close to the surface but now she had 5ks and obstacle courses as a reason to stay fit. She now realized that she could have the positive motivation of races and positive people to train with. Shannon found the perfect place when she found Journey Fitness. It is the Mission of Journey Fitness to offer fitness challenges to our members so they can see what they are now capable of outside of the gym. Shannon describes her trainers and workout buddies saying *"They are motivating and bring on a challenge when you least expect it. They know when I can push a little harder and that is when they bring over heavier weights and set them next to me or hand me a jam ball to step it up a notch"* Most importantly Shannon says *"I am a much stronger person 4 years after the first day I walked in the doors and I definitely have detoxed most of my demons."*

TAKE A JOURNEY

"When you feel like giving up, remember why you started." – Anonymous. Your greatest pain can be your greatest strength. When given the opportunity to let go of your pain and move forward take it and run with it. Run. Run. Run.

Road to Happiness

By Jeremy Purifoy and Mark Gray

"You need to make a commitment, and once you make it, then life will give you some answers."

– Lee Brown

Mark Gray

I have tried many things to better myself both physically, mentally and emotionally, but nothing ever seemed to work. My biggest challenge was commitment. Maybe I would find something that would work physically, but emotionally and mentally it did not click. Maybe it made me happy, but my body and mind did not follow suit. Then once something worked, or did not work, I would give up. I was not motivated and had no real direction or plan to obtain my goal of becoming more physically fit.

I was getting to the point in my life where I was in my 50's and was getting way too heavy and this was also weighing on my mind. I just wanted to be in better shape, mentally and physically. My emotions were at an all-time high. There was a bit of fear that if I continued gaining weight and eating very badly that I would quickly spiral down to the point of no return. I was afraid that I would not be able to do simple things in life like take a short hike, throw a football around or even walk up a flight of stairs. My weight gain even affected my day to day activities, as I noticed I was feeling more and more tired, and lacked energy. I knew I needed motivation, structure, and a strong support system.

Age has been a huge contributing factor toward my motivation and as you get older it gets harder and harder to start and maintain any type of exercise program. It is hard to fully commit to an exercise program.

During my Journey, I have established several habits and adapted different mantras; "Health is Wealth," "One Push up is Better than None," "Just Walk Through the Door," and the overall program and fitness staff at Journey Fitness has worked to motivate me to keep me coming and push myself further. Consistency has been key. When there are days that I do not want to go, I say to myself, "Just walk through the door and do something. Start with one push up and build from there." My door is Journey Fitness. I walked in and continue to walk in.

Journey Fitness gives me structured exercise circuits, nutrition classes, and empowering coaches who make me believe I can accomplish anything. No longer do I lack the motivation to make a change in my life. I look forward to coming to my workouts. I feel like I have a sense of accomplishment. I now have a much-improved outlook on life since starting Journey Fitness, I feel great!

Since I stopped second guessing, since I stopped thinking it wasn't for me, since I stopped thinking I can do it on my own, I found success! I can honestly say that I feel accomplishment when I look at myself, my progress and my outlook on life. I am on my pursuit of happiness.

TAKE A JOURNEY

Commitment and consistency is key! Give yourself 21 days to set yourself up for success. It takes 21 days to create a habit. Let day one of your 21 days be today.

EFFORT IS A CHOICE

by Jesse King

*"The best things in life are earned
by making daily deposits into the effort
account needed to achieve it."*

– Tom Ziglar.

Diabetes, heart disease, and cancer. These words can induce spine chilling sensations in even the most stoic individuals.

However, typically when we're young and relatively healthy, diabetes, heart disease, and cancer may seem rather insignificant, and not raise much of a concern. As we get older, crafty advertisements on television, in the newspaper, and on the internet, start to cause us to entertain legitimate concerns regarding our health and disease status. Our concerns become intensified and rationalized by reported skyrocketing health care costs in the news media. Truth be told, our concerns are justifiable.

The concept behind your lifestyle choice is simple. What you sow is what you reap. Just as farmers plant seeds in the Spring to harvest crops in the Fall, so do we plant seeds of either disease, or vitality which we nurture and grow through our daily choices.

Do not make the mistake of leaving the quality of your life purely to chance by making no effort towards sustaining your health and vitality. Your daily efforts do matter. Like the farmer nurturing the tiny seed daily, small things done well over time will yield better results than doing nothing at all.

But what do you do when you experience tough times - pain, set back, or frustration? In the pursuit of health and happiness, all the above will surely pay you a visit. Murphy's Law states that anything that can and will go wrong, will go wrong. Don't let this frustrating fact of life derail you from your hopes, dreams, and aspirations.

Jack Powers experienced regular frustration after going through many painful cycles of yo-yo dieting. According to Jack, "When I walked through the doors of Journey Fitness back in October 2015, even though I was not at my heaviest weight, I was indeed overweight and out of shape. I was feeling the frustration of having slowly put on weight over the past few years after I had gotten into pretty good shape in 2009. The emotions of reversing all the good I had done for myself compelled me to eat junk food that acted like a drug that would at least make me feel better for the moment. Then the guilt would set in and the cycle would continue for me to turn to very bad eating habits.

I was motivated to change because being in my mid 40's, I knew my time was limited for continuing the path I was on. Thoughts of diabetes, heart disease, and other health factors were on my mind. I knew I had to finally break the cycle I had struggled with for all of my life, and get away from yo-yo diets, and find a long-term plan for staying healthy."

Since joining Journey Fitness Jack has gone all in, committing 100% effort towards his diet, and fitness goals. As a result, Jack has lost 50 pounds at Journey Fitness. Jack is also known as the reigning MyZone champion, earning the MyZone Challenge Trophy a home at his local Journey Fitness in Ithaca. Suitably for Jack, MyZone is a heart rate monitor worn while working out that awards you effort points based on your heart rate.

Accept the facts. Some things in life are out of your control, like the weather for example. But one thing you will always have control over is amount of effort you invest into any endeavor. Make the choice to take full responsibility for your effort, and your results.

On your quest for better health, be prepared to encounter frustration. In fact, expect it. Do not let frustration keep you from fulfilling your commitments, such as working out three times a week, drinking more water, or consuming less sugar for example. The combination of effort and commitment is a powerful force used to overcome any obstacle.

Jack Powers – Before   Jack Powers - After

TAKE A JOURNEY

It's a choice to either stay the same or change. If you truly desire to make a change, it takes effort to do so. Start small by beginning to take full responsibility for your daily efforts. No excuses. Make the commitment to put forth only your best effort in everything you do. And don't stop there. Stay committed until you reach your goal. By doing so you will be putting time on your side. Let it be your ally. Small deeds done well each day lead to long term success over time.

Life Begins At The End Of Your Comfort Zone

By Travis Barnes

"This is your life, so live it."

– Kim VanSkiver

Kim VanSkiver

Kim spent most of her life never taking any chances, never really living. She did everything with a conservative approach. She was into fitness but she would always play it safe if she thought there might be a question if she could actually do something. Her insecurities always got the best of her. Then one day she was asked by her sister-in-law, Shannon, to sign up for a Half Marathon. This was definitely outside of Kim's comfort zone but because of her love for her sister-in-law she thought, "Why Not?" Kim was having a paradigm shift, and it was going to change her life.

Kim had been feeling like something was missing from her life. She felt like she had spent her whole life inside her comfort zone never really living. Normally she would have looked at this half marathon and thought, "Oh I could never do that." This time she was stretching herself. She was risking failure. She felt like this half marathon was going to be the beginning of a brand-new life, and she was right.

Besides signing up for the race, Kim did something else outside of her comfort zone. She went to Journey Fitness for an open house with Shannon so they could hear about what Journey Fitness offered for coaching. They both thought that with the help of a coach they could become stronger, more fit and run faster. After the open house, they both signed up for partner training. This also took Kim outside her comfort zone. Kim had always trained alone. The first thing her coach did is test her 1-mile run. The next thing her coach did is tell her, "We are going to treat you like a Nascar. We are going to make your body light and your engine strong." This meant Kim would drop her excess body fat and begin heavy resistance training. The training was called HIIT training, which stands for High Intensity Interval Training. This is what

Journey Fitness practices for the best strength and cardiovascular improvements.

With the encouragement of her coach, Kim tried things she had never done before. She accomplished the muscle up, which is a pull up where you actually pull yourself over the bar as if climbing over a wall. She also carried her 180-pound coach, on her back, up the local high school stadium bleachers. When race day came, Kim was more than prepared. She not only completed that half marathon with a huge sense of accomplishment, but she felt like she had begun to live.

Since that time Kim has done many more races and obstacle courses, too. With each race and each obstacle she overcomes, Kim feels a greater sense of accomplishment. She says: "I never would have imagined years ago that I would be where I am today physically and mentally. Especially mentally." Today Kim's new mantra is, "Never say Never."

TAKE A JOURNEY

If what you are doing doesn't scare you then you are not really living. Do something today that scares you. It's amazing the life you'll find waiting for you on the other side of your comfort zone.

OVERCOMING

By Jeff Case

*"Keep Learning from others
and stay positive in what you do."*

– Jim Passmore

What does 50 look like?

Well Jim Passmore can shed a little light on this subject. Jim was a fit 50-year-old man in a rut. He desperately wanted to improve his fitness level but was unable to do so with his current exercise routine. Jim struggled with sleep apnea, lower back pain and knee issues. Jim's body was screaming at him to make a lifestyle change. But like most everybody, he put it off. From digestive issues to aches and pains, Jim knew internally that he needed to maintain an active lifestyle both nutritionally and physically to climb out of this self-inflicted rut.

That's when Journey Fitness was introduced to The Hilliard Corporation, where he works. Motivational speaker, Eric

Thomas, reminds us to, "Take advantage of the opportunity, in the life-time of the opportunity." Jim was desperately needing to make a change and decided that he was going to try this and put everything into it because his time was now.

At Journey Fitness, we celebrate our clients when they hit milestones in their weight loss by putting a medal around their neck and having them wear a 20-pound vest. Jim's goal was to do just that and wear the celebrated 20-pound vest. It didn't come easily but Jim reached his goal and was medaled and vested for his workout to remind him that he doesn't want that weight back. The Journey of 20 pounds begins with a single pound.

Jim credits his success to the great personal training from Journey Fitness. The functional workouts and guidance on nutrition has kept Jim from seeing his chiropractor in months. His core has been much stronger for running and recently he just ran his fastest 5K. Jim always loves how he feels from the Journey Fitness workouts and how they have helped to alleviate the built-up stress from the day. Jim thought that his diet was good before, however he would suffer from occasional bouts with stomach discomfort. Since being with Journey Fitness Jim has learned many things but mainly how the reduction of processed carbs can have a significant impact on his stomach issues and overall health.

Jim believes that his success became real because of the encouragement on the diet, help with form with the exercises and great leadership from JC. Jim states, "JC's ability to create the energy and motivation needed for daily workouts is great. He is one of the best trainers I've ever worked with and creates great comradery with our fellow employees."

I asked Jim how he was feeling today and he said this, "I feel much stronger today and because I sit all day, my core and back feel much better when I get up. I feel that my overall health is better now. The diet and body change that I wanted to achieve at 50, I have now finally done at 53 thanks to Journey Fitness."

Always give your maximum effort when doing anything in your life. You can always push beyond what your mind is saying. Always keep learning from others and stay positive in what you do.

Jim Passamore and his trainer, JC

TAKE A JOURNEY

Change needs to be visualized before it can be achieved and realized. JC always says, "Use your vision muscles." Jim believes that this is absolutely true. The other thing Jim feels is important is, to write down your purpose and goal for this change and then take action. We are better together.

BE OPEN TO CHANGE

By Nicole Wilber

"Life is a gift, and it offers us the privilege,
opportunity, and responsibility to give
something back by becoming more."

– Tony Robbins

Joe Leonard and his family

J oe, a single father of 4, is no stranger to change. If Joe could sum his life up, prior to having children, he would use the word "selfish." His "me, myself, and I," attitude led him to make many poor, destructive choices in his life, for which he would later pay the price. Once his children came into the picture, his mindset changed. He was now responsible for 4 beautiful lives, his greatest blessings, and he knew his actions directly impacted them. This was certainly not an overnight change, but Joe's perspective gradually shifted from "me" to "them." He wanted to show his children unconditional love and determination. By making more positive choices, Joe was able to build a firm foundation for his children and in turn, rebuild a better foundation for himself.

Another major change came for Joe when he joined Journey Fitness. In his 50's now, Joe had accepted his weight and the shape he was in. He had not weighed less than 200 pounds in decades, so that being a possibility never crossed his mind. Joe reluctantly started Journey at the request of another trainer. Very skeptical, Joe was unsure of what to expect and could not imagine he would enjoy working out with a bunch of strangers. He was used to working out at other gyms and around his house, but was not very successful as far as losing weight. He was not expecting much from Journey Fitness. As he became more familiar with Journey and realized the success others have experienced, his skepticism began to fade. During his intake process, he felt that the coaches genuinely cared about him as they helped to set goals. His skepticism was now completely replaced with a game plan. Joe is now weighing in below 200 pounds and has a spot on our Wall of Fame.

Once a college athlete, it was natural for Joe to coach his kids in their sports. It was also the only way this single dad could afford to send his 4 children to a private school. Joe has and continues to serve as a positive role model for several different sports teams. He has a few lessons that are a constant no matter what sport he is coaching. His main focus for the teams is on building team unity, representing the schools and families in a positive way, and always being a good sport and respectful toward the other teams. His athletes are very disciplined and show great sportsmanship. Even if they don't realize it now, his athletes are learning important, positive lessons that they will carry on throughout their lives. One major lesson he implements in his coaching is something he has learned from Journey. Your biggest opponent is always yourself. One of the greatest rewards Joe experiences is being a positive influence for these athletes. He enjoys seeing them succeed in school and life in general.

Joe has experienced several changes throughout his life. Now he is in a much more positive, healthier place, mentally and physically, since his greatest change of all - his 4 kids. For someone who previously had a more selfish attitude, he now selflessly devotes his time and energy to changing the minds of young athletes.

TAKE A JOURNEY

Always be open to change. Change is necessary in order to grow. You never know what is possible, and who you can influence positively, if you just remain open minded.

FROM RUNNER TO RACER

By Kurtis Hall and Amy Balash

*"You must expect great things from yourself
before you can do them."*

– Michael Jordan

Amy Balash – Before and After

Running has been a part of my life since I was 8 years old. It began when my mom's friend talked about running a 5k. It sparked interest in me, and she could see that so she invited me along. I took second place that day and have been hooked ever since! Growing up as the oldest of four children the competitiveness in our house was off the charts, and getting second fueled the fire for me to keep getting better. Fast forward a few years to the fifth grade. I had been running for fun prior to but now things were becoming more official as my elementary school gym teacher started a 5th and 6th grade spring track program. I continued to run in middle school and high school training hard to get faster. I ran all year round, distance in track and then cross country as well. My senior year of high school, I was part of the first cross-country team to win a section 4 title for Horseheads, I also won the 3000m indoor track title that same year. After high school, I continued to run at Moravian College where we would go on to win the MAC championship all four years I attended in track and cross-country. I also competed in cross-country nationals my sophomore thru senior years and left college on a high note as the runner up in the MAC championships with PR's in the 10k and 5k.

My adult life rolled around and I got busy as everyone does. Married to my amazing husband Mike, with our 4 wonderful children Bryson (17), Garrison (11), Ally (10), and Carson (9) as well as teaching special education (15 years now) in the Elmira City School District. With the busy-ness of life I began to lose motivation to run/workout. I also started eating unhealthy and the results were showing on the scale. To get back on track I signed up for half marathons and tried home workout programs, but I was still unmotivated. Success wasn't coming fast enough.

My low point was when I ran my slowest half marathon ever. After seeing pictures of myself at the race, I knew something had to change and that was my motivation to get better. I joined Journey Fitness, started working on my nutrition with the help of my trainers, and I started to move in the direction I wanted to go. I began to shed time off of my half and full marathon times.

After losing 25 pounds, and getting stronger, success was the only option. It's now June of 2017 and I have successfully qualified for the 2018 Boston Marathon. I am running faster than ever before.

TAKE A JOURNEY

Surround yourself with people that will encourage you, motivate you, and push you to be the best YOU, daily!

WORK ETHIC

By Travis Barnes

*"Opportunity is missed by most people because
it is dressed in overalls and looks like work."*

– Ben Franklin

S ome things begin before we begin. I am speaking of the traits we are born with and where they come from. I wrote this book while owning 7 businesses, coaching, carrying out speaking engagements and pursuing a pilot license. Most people with one business would say that they don't have time to write a book. It's really all about work ethic and when I think of work ethic, I think of my grandfather.

My grandfather, Gene Wolcott, was 11 years old when he started his first job bagging groceries. In 9th grade his schoolteacher hit him and he responded as he puts it "by decking his teacher" and then quitting school. After quitting school my grandfather was able to fully dedicate himself to the grocery store. He tells stories of separating thousands of pounds of potatoes into 30 pound bags and carrying sides of beef bigger than he was. He says it was a long day when the big trucks would come in. I asked him once how much he made back then and he said $12.50 a week. I asked if he got overtime when he worked extra. His response was they always got paid for 40 hours but they just worked until the work was done which was sometimes 70 hours a week. Can you believe it? He worked 70 hours a week for $12.50. My grandfather's work ethic allowed him to work his way up from Meat Manager to Assistant Manager to General Manager of the whole store. It's amazing the opportunities that you find when you are willing to work for them.

I will always remember watching John Wayne movies with my grandfather. Looking back, I know the reason why he liked John Wayne was because of how much he identified with him.

"The greatness we see in others is the greatness we see in ourselves" – Larry Indiviglia.

268

John Wayne always played an honorable man who stood up for what was right and always had a strong work ethic. I remember one movie in particular- *McClintock* -where John Wayne was talking to a young man who felt embarrassed because he was down on his luck. John Wayne had just given him a job. John Wayne told him, "You were not given anything. You will give me an honest day's work and for that I will give you an honest day pay."

My grandfather repeated this line to me several times throughout my life. He always taught me to be sure to give an honest day's work for an honest day's pay. He also taught me, "If you can wake up in the morning and put your feet on the floor, then you can go to work."

TAKE A JOURNEY

So what about you? How is your work ethic? Eric
Thomas says *"Your dreams and your grind have to be
congruent. You don't want to have big dream with a small
grind."* Take time today to evaluate if the work you
are putting in is worthy of the goals you have. If you
feel you are coming up short in your nutrition or your
workouts then decide how you can do better and take
action today.

No Excuses

By Jeff Case

"Don't give in to excuses that can keep you from really living the best life God has for you."

– Joyce Meyer

Steve Chesebro

Have you ever heard of the Blown Tire Story?

Neither had Steve Chesebro until he started at Journey Fitness. Maybe you can relate. Steve was feeling tired all the time and couldn't even do his daily activities without running out of breath. He was a physical train wreck who had struggled with weight gain his whole life. Everyone he knew had struggled with weight issues so he had accepted that he was just meant to be overweight.

Wow! How many of us are feeling drained, with no self-confidence, tired most of the time and just feel like we are meant to be overweight like Steve?

When Steve started at Journey Fitness, he really did not understand what we were all about. In his first class he experienced a proper warm-up, functional fitness, and a cool down with a frozen towel that involved a relaxing and motivational story to close out the session. This story was called the flat tire story and is part of the "Language of Journey Fitness." It goes like this...

If you were riding down the road and got a flat, what would you do? You would fix it and get back on the road or call AAA, right? Exactly! No one would get out and flatten the other three tires. As it is with your diet, sometimes we can fix it. However sometimes we need to phone a friend. That could be AAA with a real-life flat tire or maybe a friend who is like-minded and shares your nutritional goal to help talk some sense back into you. At Journey Fitness, we ask that if you get a flat in your diet, like a treat that you haven't had for a while, to please get back on your diet right away instead of telling yourself that you might as well stay off your diet until Monday and you will get back on track then. This practice usually comes from an all or nothing attitude that says, "If I can't follow my diet 100% then I am a failure." We don't want 100% diet perfection. 90% is enough to see results. We don't want you to be perfect. We want you to forgive your mistakes.

Steve always refers to the "flat tire story" where he learned that the "secret" to his diet success would be his practice of getting back on track after falling off the wagon. When he would snack at night, which he claims to still do, he chooses to eat a healthy snack. Steve learned that his reason and his "Why" for better health in his life was going to be a life changing commitment. Even more importantly, it would be a Journey that he didn't have to go through alone. At Journey Fitness there are coaches, clients, family, and friends that will help you every step of the way and help to keep you on the right path. Steve proudly acknowledges his Journey Fitness family, his wife and children, and his Hilliard work family for developing a strong community of life transformers who stick by each other's side no matter what. Steve says, "It's not always easy but we take it one day at a time."

At age 58, Steve Chesebro has lost over 40 pounds with Journey Fitness. He has joined fellow members in completing a Spartan Trifecta which means completing three levels of Spartan races - Sprint, Super, and Beast. This was over 26 miles, 70 obstacles, and in more mud than you ever knew even existed. Compare the person Steve is today to the person who first walked through the doors of Journey Fitness, and he believes that he is a better person. Steve says, "I have become a better person and team player. I've learned that everyone is more equal in every way. We all have obstacles to overcome and will overcome them in different ways."

Steve's motivation to make a change is to be able to see his grandchildren grow up and graduate from school. When he retires he would like to be able to travel and see the country without worrying about medications and feeling tired. He wants to do everything he has dreamed of doing. Steve now has more confidence in himself, feels more energized and has more compassion for others. He now understands that we are all on the same Journey.

Today Steve says, "I would never have imagined, standing here today, that I would be in the physical shape I am and to have completed a Spartan Trifecta with my Hilliard Journey Fitness team. The whole experience of working harder every day toward a goal kept me motivated to do this. Watching everyone on our Team pushing themselves every day inspired me even more. It's hard to put in words the sense of accomplishment, but when we crossed the finish line, it was just overwhelming."

Take a Journey

As Steve Chesebro says, "It's easy to think of reasons not to exercise or justify eating badly but the truth is when you think of "no excuses," it brings you back into reality." Remember the 'flat tire story' and allow yourself to be less than perfect. Keep on track and No Excuses.

THE JOURNEY
CONTINUES...

THE JOURNEY CONTINUES

by Destiny Barnes

*"Your Journey is Not Your Own.
It's Much Bigger Than You."*

– Destiny Barnes

The decisions we make and actions we take can either positively or negatively impact others. It's a truth almost too simple to feel important, but if you get it then you will truly understand the ripple effect you have in this world. Your Journey is not your own. My father made a decision to give a ride to a friend, which resulted in me being without a father for 10 years while he was incarcerated. My only memories of my dad for the first 10 years of my life are from inside a prison visiting room.

For 10 years all we talked about was my father coming home and how great it would be. Anytime something was wrong, my mom would tell me that it would be better when my father came home. Then one day he did come home, but when he did he was working so hard that he still seemed absent.

Growing up without my father left me always wanting the love of a father in my life and curious what it might be like to have it. This left me curious about the opposite sex. There is a saying that goes, "curiosity killed the cat." In my case it gave me PTSD. Let me just clarify that being curious and searching for love does not mean I wanted to be sexually assaulted or raped.

In 4th grade a boy named N invited me to come over to his house. (I will use initials since I don't have permission to write about the following people.) I liked N but my parents would not have let me go. So I snuck over while my grandpa was babysitting. I thought we were going to play outside but he invited me inside to watch TV. But N had something other than TV on his mind because he put his hand on my leg and tried to climb on top of me. I was able to get away, but I was negatively impacted and hurt emotionally by the first boy I ever liked. Shortly after this, I started cutting. For me, cutting was a release. It was a way to cope with what I was feeling.

People who are sexually assaulted are three times more likely than your average person to have it happen again. In 7th grade I met my boyfriend, Z. He was a year ahead of me. I liked his dark brown hair, his not-so-deep voice, his brown eyes, the way his hair flipped and all the sports he did. He was a very popular wrestler. Z and I began to talk. We started hanging out with a group of friends. One night he called me and said, "Sneak out babe. I want to see you." I didn't want to sneak out at night or behind my parents' back. Z had to talk me into it and with a little encouragement, the next thing I knew I was at his house. He had a scary movie on and Pepsi to drink. We sat down, and he started the movie. He asked me if I wanted to lay down. Hell no! I didn't want to lie down, but after I didn't answer he started to tell me how he just wants to hold me and cuddle. I will save you the details and tell you this night ended in me being raped. It was traumatic, yet I didn't break up with him. I never told anyone what Z did so it happened more than once before we broke up. I can't explain why I didn't break up with him right away except for that I had developed a very dysfunctional relationship with the opposite sex and with each and every negative interaction my levels of depression and self-destruction grew.

One summer day, I was texting with my Uncle M. I liked him because he was my crazy uncle. He was more fun than the rest of my uncles. Uncle M was about 30 years old. He was an artist and a pot smoker who still lived at home with my Grandpa. I liked him because he would give me rides if I needed to go somewhere that I couldn't ask my parents to take me. One day I was texting with my Uncle, and he started sending me sexual photos and asked me to send some back. This time I told my mother and my mother told my father. My father wanted to kill him but we ended up pressing charges instead. This divided my family and caused me to lose several people who had been like father figures in my life including my other uncle and my grandfather.

More hurt.

More pain.

More depression.

More self-destruction.

All that had happened to me consumed me. I would play it over and over in my head. Statistics tell us that people who are sexually assaulted are also 10 times more likely to use drugs, and I began experimenting with marijuana.

My parents own Journey Fitness and routinely throw holiday parties for their staff. If the parties are at our house, they let me have a friend over as so I am not bored. It was New Year's Eve 2015 and my parents threw a party for their staff. I had a friend over, and we had been sneaking some alcohol and smoking marijuana. It was late in the evening and most of the guests had left. One of my parent's houseguest, M, was still there and he could tell I had been partying. He caught me alone and sexually propositioned me but I didn't tell my parents until the next day. My father was pissed and fired the employee who brought this guest to the party. It was scary to think that I wasn't even safe in my own home.

I felt so depressed and dirty on the inside. I was so let down by the world. People who are sexually assaulted are 33% more likely to attempt suicide. By 2017 I was in 9th grade. I was not only still cutting but also skipping school, using other drugs besides marijuana, running away, and I had attempted suicide twice. In the first three months of my 9th grade year, I had 21 days of unexcused absences from skipping school. My parents did all they could to get me back on track including driving me to school, putting me in several types of counseling, even allowing me to move in with our Pastor and going so far as to move to a different address in the hopes that changing school districts would help.

At this point you are probably questioning my parents or me. I will tell you that I never indicated I wanted a sexual relationship with any of these people. As for my parents, they are stricter than most. They sent me to the best schools, used the point system in our house and always kept me involved in positive extracurricular activities. The truth is that sometimes despite our best intentions, one decision just piles on top of another and takes us some place that we never intended to go. All the turmoil that was going on in my world was just a reflection of all the turmoil that was going on inside my soul.

I wanted to be good but it's impossible to look fixed when you are still broken. It seemed I could only be good for a short time until my destructive tendencies would creep back in. In my new school district, I stopped skipping school. I joined the Cheerleading

Team and I started getting better grades. Still I was attracted to kids, like me, who were broken. There is a saying that goes, "Tell me who your friends are and I will tell you who you are." But that is so superficial. It's not that our friends make us as much as we make our friends by searching for those who feel like we do.

My heart was troubled, and so I was attracted to troubled people. My first real friend at the new school was someone who had problems just like me. His name was B and he had also attempted suicide before. Being with B made me feel good. I felt like he was someone who could understand me.

It was St Patrick's Day weekend, when I traveled to New Hampshire with my family, that I was subjected to the 5th sexual assault of my life. I wanted to spend the night with my Aunt and Uncle because I knew they were pot smokers. What I didn't expect was that my Uncle would turn out to be a child molester. That night after my Aunt fell asleep he got in bed with me, began to touch me and tried to have sex with me. I was able to run away and escape the situation but I was not able to escape the escalating storm of pain inside me.

While trying to heal and feel safe, I ended up starting a relationship with a 20-year-old boy behind my parents' back. Being barely 15 years old, I knew that my parents would freak out but I was vulnerable and he felt safe. Then one day it all came crashing down when my dad found us together in a park. Things got physical between us all, and I ran away again. By the time the police found me, I had been cutting, and it was determined that child protective services needed to have an intervention.

This is when I was sent to Bethesda Children's Home. Bethesda was like a prison for kids. I could not leave. I tried to run twice but both times the police found me and brought me back. The environment was violent. I had fights with several of the girls and quickly had to learn to handle myself.

Perhaps my biggest challenge, was having to face my own problems. That was the real reason I wanted to run. I didn't want to face all my pain. It was too much. It was too difficult, and I just couldn't do it in a place where I felt so alone. Then I met TT who would forever change my life. TT was a counselor at Bethesda. She took a special interest in me. One night she came into my room, and we talked for hours. TT shared with me the similar things she had been through in her life. She even showed me newspaper clippings of the man who had raped her and the paper clipping showed him going to jail. She told me how she used to suffer from addiction but that she had now replaced it with running to make herself feel better. She told me that I had to stop thinking of myself as a victim and start thinking of myself as a survivor. There is a saying, "Change your thinking and you will change your life." TT's words and how she related to me inspired me to change my thinking. TT asked me to promise her that I would stop cutting, and I did. I began to exercise because of TT. I also began to want to help people like TT helped me. I only knew

TT for a couple months, and it was just a short time after that life changing conversation that TT was killed in a fatal car accident. She was the first person who I was ever close with who died. I have chosen to honor her memory by letting her positive impact last and grow. I am processing things better today. I am no longer cutting. I am helping others which also helps me, and with each passing day my relationship with my parents is improving.

My father's incarceration hurt me. Others entered my life and they have forever scarred me just for the sake of their own sick pleasure. TT made a decision to help me by talking about things that were painful to her. Pastor Scott and his wife, Lisa, made a decision to demonstrate the unconditional love of God to me by never giving up on me. My parents travel four hours each way, every weekend to spend time with me and demonstrate their love for me. It wasn't one person's decision that caused my cutting, drug use, attempted suicide or runaways. In fact, I did all those things to myself because I didn't know how to process what had happened in my life. The point is that I had some things to process, some things that I never asked for. Then one person shared something that was painful and difficult for them to share, and they did it out of love. It was because of that person that I began to heal. It was because of that person that I began to help others and I now have a story to share. I'll say it again. The decisions we make and actions we take can either positively or negatively impact others. Your Journey is not your own.

Take a Journey

There is a war that is taking place in this world between good and evil. Maybe you don't assault anyone. Maybe you just choose to wear a frown rather than a smile. Maybe someone wishes you a good day and you say, "What's so good about it?" You have the power to either positively or negatively impact others. Which will you choose?

Scriptor
PUBLISHING GROUP

WANT TO BE A PUBLISHED AUTHOR?

Scriptor Publishing Group offers services including writing, publishing, marketing and consulting to take your book...

From Dream to Published!

Email us at
info@scriptorpublishinggroup.com
to get started!